DISORGANIZED
ATTACHMENT NO MORE!

THE COMPLETE BLUEPRINT TO ACHIEVING
A SECURE ATTACHMENT STYLE IN RELATIONSHIPS

TAHA ZAID

Table of Contents

About the Author

Taha Zaid is an author and dating coach who focuses on attachment theory and how it affects relationships. He has a degree in psychology and coaching from the University of Milan. This has given him the knowledge and skills to help people navigate the dating world and find happy relationships. He is a certified dating coach who has been working in the field since 2019. He helps people understand how their attachment styles affect their relationships and how to make healthy connections. His unique approach combines his knowledge of psychology and attachment theory with real-world techniques to help people start dating, learn more about themselves, and get better at getting along with others. His coaching helps many people overcome problems and get what they want in dating and relationships, which makes him a respected figure in the coaching community. Through his writing and coaching sessions, Taha keeps giving people ideas and tools to help them find love and happiness in their relationships.

SECURELY ATTACHED BOOTCAMP

Has your relationship been lacking a secure attachment lately? Are you finding it hard to make your relationship last long?

Well, many people out ther`e experience the same and we have just the measures to help you ensure a healthy relationship!

OFFERING OUR 5 RELATIONSHIP CHANGING RESOURCES ONLY FOR YOU:

- Instant FREE access to my published bestseller books and audiobooks

- Guaranteed FREE access to my upcoming books and audiobooks

- 15 minutes FREE life altering and in-depth coaching session that you cannot miss!

- Weekly affirmations and Chat Support to aid you be on the right track

- **Join our Private Facebook Community** and connect with individuals experiencing the same and have a support circle now! Find our Facebook community by searching **"Securely Attached Bootcamp"** on Facebook OR scan the QR code below:

Introduction

Did you know that many adults travel through life carrying emotional baggage they have from infancy? It might be hard to believe, but events and circumstances from our very earliest days follow us throughout our lives – affecting our emotions, beliefs, and interactions in almost every relationship we form.

Relationships are hard, but if you're currently involved with someone or if you have ever been involved with someone, you already know that. What you might not know is that we often bring our emotional baggage along for the ride which can complicate things, and sometimes bring a relationship to an end.

Have you ever felt like life is easier for everyone else? Sometimes people seem to be living their lives in happiness and harmony while building close relationships with friends, family, and romantic partners. Meanwhile, your relationships aren't working out and you can recognize that something is off. You can even be self-sabotaging opportunities to create a loving and supportive bond with another person. While other people have long-lasting and healthy relationships, your personal experiences are much different.

Have you ever been involved with another person romantically and found that your emotions waver from being really high to being really low like a roller coaster? One day, you wake up feeling wonderful and easily able to love and accept love in return. Then, the very next day, you wake up with feelings of mistrust for your partner for no apparent reason. Perhaps you feel angry, jealous, insecure, unaccepted, fearful, or misunderstood. After stumbling through an uncomfortable day, you go to sleep feeling terrible and wondering if this relationship is even worth the amount of pain and confusion you're experiencing.

Through the night you may sleep off those feelings of discomfort and wake up the next morning feeling okay again. You may feel some remorse for your actions from the previous day and begin to justify your feelings. The next day comes and you feel the desire to seek out love from your relationship - and the cycle starts over.

If any of these scenarios sound like you, then you may be living with a disorganized attachment style. Negative experiences of physical, emotional, verbal, or sexual abuse that occurred during our earliest years can leave life-long effects that we aren't aware of.

Many people don't realize the ramifications that previous experiences can affect the way we live our lives. But the truth is, behavioral science has proven that previous experiences, going all the way back to our childhood and even early infancy, help to shape our reactions and emotions as adults. Those early childhood years are instrumental in creating the kind of adults we will become – either for better or worse.

There's plenty of science to back up this phenomenon, but what it amounts to is this – if we are allowed to feel safe, loved, and supported during our developmental years, we are better equipped to develop important coping mechanisms that are needed to function appropriately as adults. And if those things are missing from our lives as infants and children, then it's much more likely we will struggle with certain things as adults.

Disorganized attachment disorder is a condition that develops as a direct result of experiences endured as a child, or even from experiences we have later in life. And when that attachment style follows us into our relationships, it can cause chaos and disorder in our lives and with the closest people around us as well.

People with a disorganized attachment style often react unpredictably in their relationships. One minute they are seeking love and attention from their partner and the very next minute they are actively pushing them away. This type of attachment can leave people feeling extremely needy in terms of seeking a relationship and developing a truly positive, healthy bond with another person. And in the same breath, these people can be angry and fearful of that person, without having any reason for their reactions.

Living with disorganized attachment makes the possibility of maintaining a long-term relationship - based on mutual trust, respect, and love - feel almost impossible. Maybe you're the type of person who is constantly seeking this type of relationship only to find that it never lasts. Or perhaps you're in a relationship now that you feel is crumbling beneath your feet. Even if your partner is trustworthy, honest and supports you 100% of the time, you may feel unrelenting emotions of fear, distrust, and a desire to distance yourself from your partner.

Going through life feeling like you're unable to form solid relationships is a terrible feeling. Everyone deserves to feel love and trust from their partner and should be able to return those feelings without feeling unsafe. Disorganized attachment makes this a hard endeavor. You may feel the constant need to seek a positive, loving connection with another person, but then do everything in your power to avoid that closeness once it is attainable. But the good news is recognizing this fact is the first step to healing, and there is a way out. You don't have to remain stuck in these feelings forever.

This book was designed to be a solution for adults living with a disorganized attachment style, or for those who are actively loving someone who has developed a disorganized attachment style. Understanding the emotions, motivations, and reactions of those people is the first step to creating better-coping behaviors.

Recognizing patterns and attributing them to a source, then finding better ways to move forward, can make our relationships better in every aspect. There's no reason for you to continue going through life riding an emotional rollercoaster. Just because someone else didn't do a good job providing security for us when we were younger doesn't mean we are condemned to live a life where our emotions rule our actions and dictate our beliefs.

My name is Taha Zaid, and I am a life and dating coach as well as an author. My specialty is in attachment theory, and for over three years I have been advising my clients on their own relationship problems, helping them cope with those things they may not understand that are holding them back from developing a healthy and loving bond with another person.

Through the years, my clients have all testified that this coaching has truly helped them grow their personal relationships, and that's the whole reason I do this. I love what I do, which is giving the best advice to help people achieve a long-last meaningful relationship.

I deeply understand that every human being in the world is seeking a connection – and that's why helping you achieve a secure attachment with your partner matters so much to me. Even people with anxious, avoidant, or disorganized attachments can find ways to heal the inner trauma and achieve healthy attachments, and therefore sustain healthy and supportive relationships, in the future.

Healing your disorganized attachment style will be a journey – starting with some self-discovery and gaining an understanding of your own personal trauma and experiences. You will need to learn to heal that inner child and move past those traumas, learn to accept the person you have become, and most of all – learn to embrace the person you want to be. Every person deserves to experience a loving, stable relationship, and every single person out there can learn how to build the kind of relationship that makes them feel safe and healthy - a relationship where they can love and be loved.

The process can take some time and require you to develop new and improved communication skills. It might be scary to make changes that can leave you feeling vulnerable to pain and hurt, but with the best knowledge of how to develop better interpersonal skills, anyone can learn how to create positive and stable relationships.

The information you are about to learn helped me personally crack the code to having the best relationship ever, even with an insecure attachment to my partner. It was a long road, and it took about eight years for me to come to solid ground. If you're reading this, I'll bet you're a lot like me. My hope is that by reading this book and learning more about what makes you tick as a person, you can find the same peace and comfort in your own personal relationships – and maybe faster than I was able to!

This book will cover the reasons that cause people to develop insecure attachments and teach you some methods to start changing your life moving forward. After reading this book, you will understand these things clearly.

- What insecure attachments are, and how disorganized attachment can often be the most difficult style to treat

- How disorganized attachment negatively affects your interpersonal relationships

- The causes of disorganized attachment style

- How to recognize disorganized attachment in yourself and your loved ones

- How to support a partner with disorganized attachment, and how to build a better relationship with that person through supportive and loving actions

- Practical ways to overcome childhood trauma and resulting fears in your current life

- What triggers those who suffer from disorganized attachment, how to cope with the results, and how to avoid those triggers going forward

- How to build better communication skills that will facilitate an open and trusting relationship

- How to regulate the effects of your disorganized attachment, and how to potentially heal and change your tendencies so you can find the positive relationship you deserve

Now is the time to start making changes in your life – and I'm here to help you along your journey. Take the information in this book and run with it. A happier, healthier relationship is waiting for you, and you deserve every happiness life has to offer. All you have to do is get started.

Chapter 1 - How Disorganized Attachment Develops and How it Affects Your Relationships

Explaining the origins of disorganized attachment and how it affects the adult you become.

I have a close friend who has suffered from disorganized attachment their entire adult life. And while it's likely that she doesn't clearly understand the reasons for her inability to maintain a loving, healthy relationship, there's no doubt in my mind that the trauma suffered during her developmental years has a lot to do with it.

This woman lost her father at a very young age and was left to be raised by her mother and stepfather. Her mother had emotional issues of her own and was a very cold person, unable to show her the kind of love and affection she needed as an infant.

Her stepfather, meanwhile, was downright abusive - both emotionally and physically. Those early experiences led her to develop a downright mistrust of people that carried over into her adult life. And because her mother was unable to provide security, love, and a sense of safety for her, she spends a lot of time seeking those things from her adult relationships.

The problem is, even when she is able to find a partner that is loving, honest, and supportive in every way, she eventually pushes them away. She runs hot and cold, sometimes coming off as very loving and approachable, and other times feeling angry, and distant. Her emotions derived from that internalized fear of abuse and anger caused her to flee from relationships before those feelings could occur again. And yet, she continually looks for relationships that might fill that emotional void.

This is a common scenario for a lot of us living through our adult years. We are constantly seeking the perfect relationship - one that will help us feel safe and loved and able to be our true selves in every way. Simultaneously, we are finding every reason not to continue these relationships because of the fear of being hurt again. Some people even seek out relationships that they know are toxic or choose partners who are likely to be carbon copies of those caregivers who hurt them so badly as infants. At least that way they know what to expect from that person and are able to better cope with the fallout.

The good news is that even if this story is relatable to you - it doesn't have to stay that way! A little knowledge goes a long way and learning about the factors that motivate our actions is the first step in changing those actions going forward.

Attachment Styles – Secure and Insecure Relationships

There are two main categories of attachment styles – secure and insecure. Those people with a secure attachment style were raised by caregivers who were present, engaged, and able to respond to an infant's needs in a predictable way. Those infants receive the kind of support and positive interactions with adults that allow them to grow into well-adjusted adults.

When you have a secure attachment style, you are able to engage in relationships and feel entirely safe doing so. You avoid attachments with people that demonstrate toxic behaviors and seek out positive, healthy relationships instead.

Insecure attachment styles develop as a result of negative interactions with our primary caregivers as infants. There are three insecure attachment styles:

- Anxious (or preoccupied) attachment

- Avoidant (or dismissive) attachment

- Disorganized (or fearful-avoidant) attachment

People with an anxious attachment style typically grew up with caregivers who were neglectful or unpredictable in their care. A pattern of neglect and uneven responses from caregivers leads to adults who feel the need for constant reassurance in their relationships and may be overly clingy and demanding of attention.

In my book, *Anxious Attachment No More*, I discussed in depth the anxious attachment style and how it develops from our childhood experiences with neglectful and inconsistent caregivers. I also offer practical advice for overcoming the anxious emotions that stem from this style of attachment and solutions for those people striving toward a secure attachment style in their relationships.

The avoidant attachment style is characterized by adult behaviors that, at first glance, seem like positive qualities, such as extreme independence and self-sufficiency. The problem is those qualities bleed over into emotional bonds, and the adult with an avoidant attachment will have a hard time sharing their feelings.

This behavior stems from having caregivers who reject those same emotional needs as infants. The infant learns that sharing their needs by showing emotion is unlikely to elicit any response from caregivers, so they stop trying.

The avoidant attachment style is a topic I covered in my book, *Avoidant Attachment No More*. In this book, I explained the roots of avoidant attachment and how it stems from caregivers who fail to respond to our needs as infants. I also explain how to break down those walls that people with avoidant attachment build around themselves, so they can finally feel comfortable getting close to someone and learn to return that love in a healthy way.

Disorganized attachment style, like all attachment styles, typically develops during our early childhood and infancy. It is directly related to our experiences and interactions with our primary caregivers. Disorganized attachment is often considered the most difficult of the three attachment styles to treat because it shares characteristics with both anxious and avoidant attachment styles.

Infants with a disorganized attachment style likely had to endure caregivers who were abusive, either physically, emotionally, or sexually. Or perhaps they witnessed their caregiver actively abusing someone else, or they were subjected to trauma of some kind. The biggest driver of behaviors related to disorganized attachments is fear.

Infants with a disorganized attachment style learn that caregivers are unreliable, untrustworthy, and unsafe - but yet they simultaneously seek these attachments. They crave love, attention, and safety, and may reach out for it on occasion. But they will also recoil as a reaction to prior experiences where the caregiver has responded with anger. These are beliefs that are carried over into adulthood and then applied to adult relationships as well.

Infants rely entirely on their caregivers for everything - food, safety, shelter, love, attention, and knowledge of how the world works. And, instinctively, babies understand that. Their entire world revolves around those caregivers for the first several years of their lives, and they build an understanding of how people interact with each other, and what to expect during those interactions, along the way.

A baby cries to elicit a response from a caregiver. It could be related to hunger, pain, fear, or simply to get the caregiver's attention. That crying behavior, in a supportive environment, will likely result in some kind of response from the caregiver. If the baby is hungry, the baby receives food. If the baby is in pain or fear, the baby receives comfort and love.

But what happens when the infant doesn't get the kind of response expected? When the person who is supposed to be the primary source of comfort, love, and support for an infant responds to that infant's needs with anger or reacts inconsistently, the infant internalizes that as a typical response and will carry those expectations into adult relationships.

What Causes Disordered Attachment Style

Infants that develop a disordered attachment style often suffered abuse, neglect, and trauma at an early age. There could be a combination of these things that contributed to the development of this insecure attachment, or it could stem from one, very traumatic and formative experience.

Causes of Disorganized Attachment

- Physical abuse

- Emotional abuse

- Verbal abuse

- Sexual abuse

- Having a caregiver who responds with anger

- Having a caregiver who abuses someone else

- A traumatic experience stemming from infancy or early childhood

When infants experience these types of abuse at such a vulnerable and developmental stage of their lives, it creates a ripple effect. They internalize this abuse and build unconscious expectations of how every future relationship will play out.

Remember that infants only know one thing – that their caregiver is their only source of comfort and safety. They rely on that caregiver for everything, and they learn how to cry out for it when they are in need.

Disorganized attachment starts to develop as soon as the infant learns that asking a caregiver to meet their basic needs is met with anger and negative behaviors.

When a baby wants attention, they cry. Sometimes they even scream uncontrollably until a caregiver notices their distress. At such a young age, and without the benefit of language at their disposal, it's the only tool babies have. And anyone who has ever raised a child of their own knows babies aren't afraid to use their lungs to get attention when they need something.

In a typical upbringing, with a caring, attentive, and supportive caregiver, that child receives a positive response due to them crying out. The caregiver approaches them, probably speaking in a soft tone, picks them up, cradles them in their arms, and takes whatever action is necessary to calm and soothe the baby - whether that is changing a wet diaper, getting a bottle ready, or simply holding the baby close to their body.

All of these positive reactions build secure attachments that are carried over into adulthood. The infant learns that it's okay to ask for a caregiver to meet their needs, and that doing so will result in a positive interaction and actually having those needs met. There is no anger in response to the request from the infant. There is no smacking, yelling, hitting, or even ignoring that happens when the baby cries. Every scenario has a happy ending, and the baby feels a constant sense of security and safety when reaching out for love and attention.

In the opposite scenario, the infant cries out to a caregiver who is unable to respond positively. It could be because the caregiver lacks the skills or coping mechanisms to react appropriately. It might relate to abuse or neglect that occurred in the caregiver's own infancy which has created a vicious cycle of abuse. Or it could be a result of stress, depression, anxiety, or substance abuse on the part of the caregiver.

Whatever the cause, the result is that the baby cries out for its needs to be met and is given a negative response as a consequence. The baby learns that asking for love and attention runs the risk of pain and fear in return - and will develop a persistent correlation between the two things. They seek for their needs to be met - but fear the response they will get because they have learned to expect a negative reaction.

How Disorganized Attachment Affects Your Relationships

The term "relationship" can be defined as the way in which two or more objects, concepts, or people are connected. People in a romantic relationship exist in a state of connection - relying on each other, relating to each other, and communicating with each other.

There are other types of relationships apart from romantic connections. We develop relationships with our family members. We build relationships with friends and acquaintances. We even have relationships with bosses and coworkers. Each of these types of relationships looks very different and includes a different dynamic. You wouldn't expect the relationship with coworkers to look or feel the same as the relationship with a romantic partner, and vice versa (at least hopefully not. If you do – that's an entirely different book!)

But despite their differences, the way in which we react and respond to these relationships, and the people involved in them, often stem from similar experiences. If we have a common mistrust of people in the workplace or have been wronged by close friends – it's likely those feelings of hurt and mistrust will manifest themselves somewhere in our other relationships. Those experiences don't go away. Instead, they can dictate our emotions and behaviors with other people, even if we don't immediately realize it.

Many times, our relationships are at the mercy of our unconscious responses and behaviors. We might not even realize the extent to which it's happening. And it's not just our romantic relationships that suffer because of it – but every interaction that happens between ourselves and someone else.

Every encounter with another person leaves us vulnerable, even if we are secure and stable. When you interact with someone else, you are at the mercy of their behavior. Of course, how you choose to react and respond is very much under your control, and learning how to respond in a healthy way to negative encounters is important. Those people we interact with regularly may be suffering from their own insecure attachment style that is affecting their behavior in return.

Our attachment style, whether secure or insecure, has a huge effect on the way we approach, build, and maintain our interpersonal relationships. A disorganized attachment style leads to attention-seeking behaviors combined with avoidance behaviors. We want a connection, but we fear that connection. We want to ask for love, but we fear the response we will get from partners. Living life this way is unpleasant in the least, and potentially crippling at its worst.

What Disorganized Attachment Looks Like in a Relationship

Disorganized attachment is one of the most complicated types of attachment styles because it combines elements from other attachment styles. It's unpredictable and unstructured. It can often feel like there is no rhyme or reason for the actions taken by someone with a disorganized attachment.

People with a disorganized attachment style have developed an unconscious expectation of how people in their lives will react to their need and desire for a true, loving connection with that other person.

Another term for disorganized attachment style is the "fearful-avoidant" style. And looking at the meaning of these two words, it is easy to see how those emotions that developed as infants can affect us as adults.

Infants reach out to their primary caregivers for love and affection, and to have their basic needs met. They have no other options at such a young age and are completely at the mercy of those caregivers. Infants must have their needs met in order to feel safe and secure.

When the primary caregiver responds to an infant's outcry to have these needs met with anger or abuse - it creates a situation where the infant is afraid of reaching out for those things in the future. And that feeling of fear and uncertainty can bleed over into adulthood.

A partner who has disorganized attachment truly wants to develop a healthy connection, but because of those early childhood traumas, they are afraid to do so. They have learned to expect that when they ask for love and attention, they get anger and abuse in return.

Adults with disorganized attachment often experienced caregivers who were inconsistent in the way they responded to their needs as infants. They could have received love and security on some days, or they may have gotten a response that was negative instead of positive.

This differs from the avoidant attachment style, because those infants never received any love or attention from their caregivers, and so stopped seeking it altogether. And it differs from the anxious attachment style because people who experience this type of attachment are typically constantly seeking reassurance and affection from their partners to the extent of becoming overly clingy or needy.

Disorganized attachment can look a lot like both anxious and avoidant attachment. Or it can look like neither. That's because adults with disorganized attachment are exactly that - disorganized. They crave love, safety, and affection from their partners, but are unable to trust that those things will be offered without having negative consequences like anger attached to them. So they seek and avoid at the same time.

This can leave people who are in a relationship with someone who has a disorganized attachment style feeling bewildered and uncertain. Their partner may be loving, happy, and lighthearted one minute, and then cold and angry the very next moment. It can be hard to understand these reactions, especially if the partner in question feels like they're offering a truly open, healthy, and supportive connection.

It doesn't feel good to have a partner who runs hot and cold seemingly for no reason. And without an understanding of the reasons a partner is behaving that way, it can mean the early end to even the best relationships. However, if you're able to understand how those early childhood experiences and traumas are affecting your partner all these years later, then you can develop coping methods and communication skills that can help both partners move forward in a healthy way.

Once you understand what to look for – either in yourself or in a close partner – it might seem obvious that disorganized attachment is causing most of the disharmony in a relationship.

Some common effects of disorganized attachment are:

- An extreme need to feel close to someone followed or combined with a tendency to reject that closeness

- Pushing people away

- Chaotic or unpredictable patterns involving interpersonal relationships – acting very hot then very cold toward a partner

- Lashing out at partners or exhibiting overly aggressive behavior or responses

- Displaying unwarranted fear of partners or companions

- Low self-esteem and a negative self-image

- Depression, anxiety, or emotional imbalances

- Feeling ashamed, unworthy, unlovable, or insecure

- Often paired with other emotional disorders, such as borderline personality disorder

- Can be accompanied by substance abuse, alcohol dependency, or self-harm behaviors

All of these things can develop in response to a disorganized attachment style. And just looking through the list, it's easy to see how damaging the effects of this phenomenon can truly be. Going through life with feelings of low self-esteem, depression, and anxiety is something nobody wants to experience, and you shouldn't need to feel stuck in these patterns.

Now that you have a clear understanding of what disorganized attachment style is, how it develops, and how it can drastically affect your relationships – it's time to learn what you can do about it.

These things that build up from our infancy are not permanent. Yes, they are heavily ingrained into our subconscious – so much so that we probably don't even realize it, but there is hope. We can actively work to change our fear response going forward so that we don't end up sabotaging every possibility to build a positive relationship.

We can look back at those early childhood experiences and learn from them. Understanding exactly what happened to you as an infant and how those experiences contributed to who you have become as an adult is the first step in figuring out how to change those behaviors.

In the following chapters, we will look at some tools that you can use to learn better coping mechanisms, learn how to heal those inner traumas, and develop better communication skills. With these things, you will be able to manage your disorganized attachment in a more sustainable way, or even figure out how to reverse it altogether. Keep reading and let's get into the real work!

Chapter 2 – The 'I Hate You, Stay With Me' Syndrome

How to love and enjoy your relationship when your partner has a disorganized attachment style.

We can now understand that having a disorganized attachment style has a direct impact on how we respond to our partners in a relationship. So, let's talk some more about what that's like for the other partner in that type of relationship.

Having a romantic partner who is living with disorganized attachment can be a struggle. It may seem insurmountable on occasion, and there will likely be times when you wonder if the hassle is even worth the effort. After all, you probably feel like you're not giving your partner any reason to react the way they do. You're not a cheater, you're not an abuser, and you're not controlling. You don't yell or call your partner names in anger. You don't throw things across the room during arguments or discussions. You make yourself as available as possible in every way, and yet still, your partner pulls away from you.

You might be left wondering, "what else can I do here?" And that's an understandable response. If it feels like you're the only half of the partnership making an effort to better the situation and solve problems, it will likely start to feel overwhelming and fruitless.

What's to be done? It depends greatly on how self-aware your partner is about their issues. Do you have a partner who says outright, "I have disorganized attachment and I often react unpredictably because of it"? Or do you have a partner who has no understanding of the reason for their behavior?

If the former is true, and you have a partner who understands the reasons behind their insecure attachment style, then you're already halfway there. You have already won half the battle to find solutions that can help both of you cope with the fallout of this issue, and work together to build a better relationship moving forward.

If the latter is true, then you must read carefully. It will likely do more harm than good to point a finger at your partner and make them feel as if the problems are all their fault. In truth, they probably already feel that way, even if they don't fully realize it. But don't despair if this is the case. There are subtle ways that you can address the issue with your partner and working on open and honest communication is one of the best tools at your disposal to do so.

This chapter will help you understand what it's like to live with a partner who struggles with disorganized attachment. We will discuss how to show love and support to that person as they navigate powerful and often overwhelming emotions. And I will offer practical tips and strategies you can start using today that will help you both along your journey. The fact that you're reading this book in an effort to better understand your partner's needs and find solutions to help them feel safe, happy, and loved speaks volumes about how much you care about that partner. Together, we can figure this out so that your relationship with your partner can become the best it can be.

Loving Someone with Disorganized Attachment – What it Looks Like

I recently rewatched the 1998 blockbuster movie *Good Will Hunting*, starring Matt Damon and Robin Williams. If you've never had the chance to watch it, I highly recommend it, not just for the stellar performances and captivating storyline – but because Matt Damon's character in the movie is a perfect example of someone who is struggling with disorganized attachment.

Matt Damon's character, Will Hunting, is a rough-and-tumble troublemaker from South Boston who just happens to be a mathematical genius. When his genius is discovered, he is rescued from jail by a professor and sent to a psychologist, played by the amazing Robin Williams. The character of Will Hunting has trust issues, evidenced by his choice of a few very close friends who cannot compete with him intellectually, and therefore do not represent a threat. He has trouble regulating his emotions and lashes out during confrontations, either physically or by verbally assaulting the other party. This is especially displayed in his visits to numerous psychologists before eventually being sent to Sean, the psychologist played by Williams, as a last resort. Will uses his intelligence to disarm them, ridicule them, and eventually cause them to walk away – never actually walking away himself.

William's character is the down-to-earth psychologist who shares a commonality with Will – he also suffered abuse as a child. Sean hails from the same neighborhood, and they both have a love of literature and weightlifting. At first, Will tries to push Sean away - just like everyone else he encounters. But Sean is slowly able to connect with Will, showing him what a secure relationship looks like, both in their interactions and his stories about his relationship with his own wife.

Throughout the course of the movie, Damon's character falls in love with a young lady named Skylar, exhibiting every desire to be with her. The problem is that Skylar represents a threat to Will because she is highly intelligent like him and actively wants to build a relationship. When that relationship starts to become something serious, it leaves Will feeling vulnerable. When his attachment issues finally cause a blowup, he decides it's safer for his well-being if he ends the relationship.

During the pivotal scene, where Will and Sean are looking through the young man's "file," filled with disturbing images of the physical abuse he suffered while in the foster care system, Will breaks down. He first becomes angry and confrontational, pushing Sean away, and then openly sobs as Sean repeats the phrase, "It's not your fault."

Just before that revelation, Will asks Sean what the file says – even asking him if the file says he has "attachment issues." It's clear from the story that Will suffered terrible abuse during his years in the foster care system. The abandonment he feels from being orphaned, and the subsequent attachment issues he develops as a result of the abuse suffered from those adults who were charged with his care is evident, especially in his push and pull towards and away from Skylar's love.

This is a great example of what it's like to live with and love someone with a disorganized attachment. In the movie, Skylar truly cares for Will and expresses how much she wants to understand him and help him find ways to cope. But in the end, her desire to be the Band-Aid for his issues isn't enough, and Will flees from her rather than risk potential hurt. He's afraid of the pain that he thinks love will cause because that's all he's known up to this point. In order to move forward, he has to come to the realization that, 1: it's not his fault, and 2: love doesn't have to hurt.

In the end, Will leaves Boston to chase after Skylar, deciding that the risk of hurt is trumped by the possibility of a healthy, wonderful relationship.

Dating someone with a disorganized attachment can be challenging, and sometimes you might feel like giving up. But if your partner is willing to work through their issues, and you, like Skylar, are willing to be the support system they need to do so, then there is hope for a better future for the both of you.

Your Partner – and Their Disorganized Attachment

Maintaining a relationship with someone who has attachment issues can sometimes feel like there are actually three individuals in the relationship instead of two - you, your partner, and their attachment disorder.

That's because your loved one is more than the sum of their emotional responses. And they likely have good days and bad days - or even a string of good moments followed by a breakdown and a long period of negative moments. It can feel like riding a rollercoaster, but one where you can't see where the road ahead lies. You can't prepare for the next hill or drop, because the path is dark and unknown. All you know, likely from past experience, is that the drop is coming eventually.

Living in that constant state of expectation, where the expectation is an emotional confrontation that you have little control over, can be exhausting. And if this scenario continues to play repeatedly over a period of months or years, it can be easy to become resentful towards your partner. Without proper perspective, it might feel like they simply thrive on the drama created by their mood swings. You might develop a mistrust of their true feelings because even when they say they love you and want to be with you, you might be holding your breath in anticipation of the next swing from happy to angry, distant, and avoidant.

How is one supposed to manage these fluctuating feelings? The first step is understanding what is causing your partner's reactions in the first place. Since we have previously explained that disorganized attachment develops as the result of traumatic childhood experiences, abuse, or a caregiver who is unable to regulate their own emotions, it should be understood that your partner is not like this through a choice of their own. They did not choose to have a disorganized attachment, but rather developed it unknowingly and unwillingly, possibly as far back as infancy. It's not something they did, but something that was done to them by others.

Truly understanding this fact will lead to you being able to develop empathy for your partner's situation, and even potentially put yourself in their shoes. It's an internalized fear of pain, hurt, and rejection that is causing them to act the way they do. It's not their fault, and it's not yours either.

Common Disorganized Attachment Traits

If you're unsure if your partner has a disorganized attachment style, consider the common characteristics exhibited by individuals who struggle with this issue. But remember that everyone is different, and your partner may share one or two of these traits, but not all of them.

- Has trouble forming long-lasting relationships with others

- Struggles with forming emotional bonds with others

- Subconsciously sabotages relationships

- Displays jealousy and distrust even when it's unwarranted

- Exhibits severe mood swings and emotions, going from hot to cold very quickly

- Often overgeneralizes or overanalyzes situations, and overdramatizes their responses

- Reacts with extreme behavior when they feel hurt by something

- Provokes others in situations to cause a confrontation, but doesn't take any responsibility for the conflict

- Often holds a grudge for a long time

- Seeks to punish those they feel have wronged them by withholding attention or through other actions

- Can come across as manipulative or exhibit what seems like "gaslighting" behavior

- Becoming emotionally unavailable, cold, and detached

- Can seem overly attentive, needy, and loving at times

- Has a hard time opening up about their feelings or experiences

This list of character traits all stems from disorganized attachment, a direct result of experiences from infancy and childhood that caused your partner to internalize the idea that love hurts. In reality, they want an open and healthy relationship, but as soon as the possibility of that happening becomes too real, their inner voice tells them that danger lies ahead.

This feeling causes a sort of internal panic that can lead to behavior designed to push other people away, even if it's done subconsciously. They might try to justify their behavior by bringing up faults in others or concocting scenarios where it seems to make sense for them to get as far away as possible, without ever taking any responsibility for the issue.

To understand the motivations behind these actions, let's look at some of the internal emotions your partner with disorganized attachment is feeling.

- Fear

- Loneliness

- Anxiety

- Low self-esteem

- Low self-worth

- Feelings of regret

- Feelings of depression and sadness

- A sense of inevitable doom and impending disaster

- Feeling out of control

- Feeling like giving up

Looking through this list of emotions, it can be easier to see the direct correlation between how your partner with disorganized attachment is feeling and how they actually behave.

I Hate You – Please Don't Leave!

A common pattern exhibited by individuals with disorganized attachment is the "I hate you – Stay with me" syndrome. This perfectly describes the rollercoaster of emotions your partner is likely feeling.

The "I hate you" part comes from a place of fear and anxiety. Being in a truly open and honest relationship can be scary, even for those of us with a secure attachment. There's a vulnerability that must come along with complete honesty and transparency. When you and your partner are able to expose every part of yourself to each other without fear of any judgment or negative reaction, then you have figured out the balance of a perfectly healthy relationship.

For the person with disorganized attachment, however, that place of vulnerability is a well-known experience for them. The problem is they have associated that feeling with pain and fear because of a learned, internal response. As infants, they reached out for that love, and in return they were offered abuse, anger, pain, and resulting fear. So now, every time those feelings of vulnerability start to creep too close to the surface, they push away to prevent what they feel is the inevitable pain that will follow.

The "stay with me" half of the syndrome is what makes disorganized attachment one of the more complicated and harder-to-heal attachment styles. It's what causes the see-saw effect – the rollercoaster ride – the hot and cold emotions that seem to come so often. They truly want a deep emotional connection with another person. As infants, they may have even received that kind of attention, but in an unreliable manner. Or maybe they never received it, and so they reach for it even more.

Disorganized attachment is a confusing mixture of anxious and avoidant attachment styles. So even though your partner will find ways to push you away, over and over again, they will try to pull you back in just as strongly. And they will never admit that it's fear causing this see-saw behavior because they don't realize it themselves. It's merely a self-preservation tactic that has developed because they have learned to associate a loving relationship with future hurt and pain.

It's also one of the big reasons that many individuals with disorganized attachment are drawn to partners who also have an insecure attachment style. And those people are drawn to them in return – the like attracts like theorem. Two people with insecure attachment styles in a relationship is a dynamic that will likely lead to an explosion – or an implosion. The on-again, off-again emotions will create a back-and-forth between the two that only serve to fuel the behavior and cause a cycle of dysfunction that cannot be sustained.

How to Love a Partner with Disorganized Attachment

There are some things that you can do if you're struggling to balance a relationship with someone who has a disorganized attachment. These tips apply to all kinds of relationships, not just romantic ones. Friendships and relationships with family members can suffer as a result of this dynamic as well. And everyone deserves happy, healthy relationships in all aspects of their lives, including with a romantic partner.

Below are some of my best tips for supporting someone with disorganized attachment. These are things that you can easily do every day to help that person feel safe and secure. There must be a disclaimer here though – don't expect a complete turnaround overnight, even if you try your very best to employ every one of these tips. Your partner has carried these feelings of fear and distrust with them for a lifetime, and it will take patience, practice, and a good amount of time and reinforcement to change their way of thinking.

COMMUNICATION IS KEY

This fact is true in every relationship – and even more so when someone has a disorganized attachment. Your partner has learned that love, connection, and intimacy go hand in hand with vulnerability, and as a result, often finds ways to feel safe as soon as those feelings start to surface.

Chances are they are lacking the communication skills to express these feelings to anyone else and may not even understand them entirely themselves. Even if they do understand the reasoning behind their behavior and responses, there may be an internalized fear of the response they will get if they share them with someone else.

Keeping emotions and feelings bottled up is an unhealthy coping mechanism. In the case of disorganized attachment style, it can be the result of the unhealthy child-caregiver relationship they endured as an infant. When an infant cries, it's a direct action meant to elicit a response from a caregiver to meet a very real need – it could be hunger, pain, fear, or any other need an infant relies on their caregiver to fulfill.

Infants rely on many cues from the adults around them to gauge their safety. Soothing voices, soft faces, gentle touches, and being held close to the body are all reactions to an infant's cries that provide a sense of calm. Couple that with a caregiver who reliably meets a child's needs - and you wind up with a child who learns to trust the adults around them and an ability to gauge the response they will get from crying. These infants are able to build a secure attachment, and likely learn the ability to communicate without fear of repercussion.

When a child gets a negative response to those cries, whether it's an angry look, a loud, yelling voice, physical abuse, or neglect by the caregiver failing to meet the child's needs, it has the opposite effect. That infant learns that asking for their needs to be met, or openly communicating those needs to someone else, will result in a negative response. They associate those negative responses with reaching out for safety - and learn to associate a fear of rejection and an anger response with open communication.

The result is that individuals with disorganized attachment fear sharing their feelings with anyone else. Because they have learned that sharing their feelings or expressing a need only ends up with them feeling pain, fear, and shame.

Building an open line of communication between two people takes work and practice. You can start to build that bridge of trust by sharing your own feelings with your partner, showing them that opening yourself up is possible and can happen without an ensuing negative reaction. Don't push them to do the same until they are comfortable doing so, because they will likely draw back even further. But consistently offering to listen when they're ready to share will let them know the door is open, and you represent a safe space when the time is right.

FOLLOW THROUGH – EVERY TIME

A disorganized attachment style is closely related to feelings of insecurity. Infants who experience abuse or neglect were never able to find consistent feelings of safety and security, instead experiencing adults who failed to react expectedly. This uneven and inconsistent response typically results in an anxious attachment style. But those with a disorganized attachment style experience the worst of both worlds. Their caregivers were inconsistent to the point of responding with anger and violence at some points, instead of just neglect.

Inconsistency in your actions and responses is sure to be a trigger for your loved one with disorganized attachment. When you say you're going to do something, or promise to show up somewhere, then do so - every time - without fail. This will help build an important trust relationship for your partner, instead of reinforcing their already held beliefs that people are not to be trusted.

Another way to be consistent is through your responses themselves, something that can be challenging when dealing with a partner who has trouble regulating their own emotions. It can be tempting to respond to extreme outbursts of anger by becoming angry yourself. It can be hard to respond with a calm voice and a gentle demeanor when someone is railing at you, spitting insults and accusations. But, if you make an effort to do so, you help your partner build a sense of security and safety instead of underlining their expectations. Remember, they expect those who claim to love them to react in anger and cause them pain – so make every effort not to do so.

BE PATIENT AND EMPATHETIC

Learning to change long-held behaviors that result from early-childhood experiences is a journey, not a short jaunt. So your partner can't be expected to make a 180 in a few short days, or even weeks. Depending on the severity of the abuse experiences your partner lived through, their understanding of their own trust issues, and their willingness to work on balancing their emotions, it could take years before they can feel one hundred percent safe in a relationship. If you expect to be around for the long term, then that has to be okay with you as well.

It can be hard to remain patient all the time, especially when faced with extreme emotions from a partner. At times, it may seem like they are trying everything in their power to get you to throw in the towel or act out in an extreme manner yourself. Either response from you would give them exactly what they expect, and just what they think they need – to cause a relationship to end before they can get hurt.

Instead, in those moments when you start to feel overwhelmed or like you might say something hurtful out of frustration, try to take a few deep breaths and start over. Leaving the situation might seem like a good idea, and if things ever start to turn violent, of course, your safety is important and you should remove yourself. However, if you can show patience with your partner and exhibit understanding and empathy for their feelings, it will create a sense of security and trust for them in return.

BE READY TO LISTEN

Remember when I said communication is key? Well, it's true, and if you are going to try and build a relationship with an open line of communication, then you must also be ready to listen when your partner is ready to speak.

Listening actively is a skill that sometimes takes practice. But it's vitally important that when your partner starts to open up about their feelings, fears, and emotions, you respond with an attentive demeanor and your full attention. Doing or saying anything that would undermine that progress will negate all the hard work it took to get to this place.

Once you have listened to what your partner has to say, offer reassurances to help them understand when their fears are unwarranted or irrational. This is an important first step for helping your partner unlearn their internalized fear and reinforce a newly learned pattern of behavior, one where they are safe even when they expose themselves to someone else.

For example, if your partner expresses a fear or concern that you're going to cheat on them or leave them for someone else, gently point out that those are actions you have never taken in the past, so there should be no reason to suspect them of you in the future.

SEEK PROFESSIONAL HELP

Sometimes there is only so much we can do as loving partners, friends, or family members. There may come a time when the individual with a disorganized attachment would benefit from seeking professional therapy or counseling.

The person may be resistant to such a suggestion, especially at first. But on the other hand, they may express an immediate interest in the idea. Having the opportunity to speak openly to a therapist can feel like a neutral ground for many trauma survivors. They will likely be more willing to open up to someone like this because there is an understanding that they won't receive ridicule, anger, or violence in return.

Therapy can be very rewarding for many people, especially those who suffered from negative childhood experiences. Depending on your partner's needs, and your own, you could even consider couple's therapy, which can be a beneficial tool for both of you to use to find solutions and pathways forward in a healthy, positive way.

How to Live Happily Ever After When Your Partner Has a Disorganized Attachment Style

Living happily ever after is an ideal we all strive for in our relationships. And it can be attained, even when your partner struggles with disorganized attachment. But – and this is a big but – it will take work, patience, and understanding from both of you.

Here are some tips to remember as you work on bettering your relationship.

- Actively work to understand the person's reactions and behaviors

- Find ways to demonstrate your love and affection

- Communicate with each other, and listen when the other person expresses a need

- Respond with calmness and patience when the other person is experiencing strong emotions

- Be cognizant of your facial expressions, tone of voice, and body language

- Recognize the person's boundaries, and don't push them past their own comfort level

- React consistently and follow through with commitments

Do these things, and take the time to work through conflicts, and you will have the chance to build the kind of relationship you truly desire - and the kind of connection you and your partner, friend, or loved one absolutely deserves.

Chapter 3 – You Only Live Once

Practical ways to overcome your fear, handle your childhood trauma, and live in the moment.

We have learned that a disorganized attachment style is a result of trauma, abuse, and negative experiences with our caregivers as infants and young children. The behaviors that result from disordered attachment might seem to come from a million different directions and stem from many different emotions, and in essence – they do. But it really comes down to one thing – fear.

Those early childhood experiences likely happened a long time ago, but the effect they have on our development is long-lasting. Those experiences shaped our expectations and understanding of the world around us and taught us what kind of reactions we can expect from the people who surround us.

If those experiences were loving, and supportive, and helped us grow up feeling safe and secure, then we turn into adults who exhibit those same characteristics. We are able to show love to other people and accept love in return without that creeping uncertainty and fear of rejection or harm. We don't get that fight or flight response that is triggered by closeness and intimacy, instead, we feel a sense of peace and tranquility. Loving someone entirely and being able to feel loved in return is one of the greatest experiences in life, and those individuals struggling with the emotions left over after childhood trauma have been robbed of those feelings.

We are left feeling like every scenario is an opportunity for disaster, because we have seen it happen before. As an infant, we knew no other truth. Love, emotion, connection, and intimacy are things to be avoided, especially when they start to get too close to our inner "safe space." That's when we look to find a way out - an escape. Better to get out than get hurt again.

Try as we might, those feelings seem to creep in every time things start to get good. Even when everything seems to be going well, and our partner is honest, responsive, understanding, and loving - that little voice in the back of our minds starts to speak up, whispering doubts into our heads.

"You're going to get hurt again."

"They don't really love you."

"You can't trust them."

"You're not good enough."

"You don't deserve that kind of love.'

"They're going to leave you."

"How do I get them to stay?"

All of these questions can become a part of our internal dialogue when we have a disorganized attachment style. Because in reality, we want love. We really want that connection with another human being. But, the other half of us, existing at the exact same moment, knows only that there is hurt and pain in the future. That leads us to find some way to avoid that hurt, even if it means pushing away, or blaming the other person for pushing away when they're not.

So, is there a way out? How do we heal from our childhood trauma and move past it to create a better person today? It can be done, but it will take a lot of work and dedication to the task. And you have to move through the process at your own pace.

There's no magical formula to healing childhood trauma, and no two people will have an identical experience. Every single person who suffered a terrible childhood likely encountered different experiences. Our environments were different, and our caregivers were different, and therefore, the outcomes are different.

Just like snowflakes, each of us is unique. The same is true of our past experiences. And each twist and turn we took along the way led us down a different road and changed the person we became as an adult.

So it only makes sense that every person's journey to becoming a more whole and healthy person will look different. Every individual will need to uncover their own past traumas and find healthy coping mechanisms to help him or her move forward. Each person's path to recovery will look very different and will move at its own pace. And that's perfectly okay.

Fighting Your Fears

The first step to overcoming the feelings that build up from childhood trauma is finding ways to handle stress and fear. Like everything, those fears go all the way back to our earliest childhood days.

In the field of mental health, there is a therapy technique called "exposure therapy." The idea of exposure therapy is to get a person who has developed an unwarranted or unjustified fear of something to encounter that thing - over and over again - until they're no longer afraid of it.

This type of immersive therapy is often used with individuals who have an obsessive-compulsive disorder. These people have irrational fears related to obsessive or repetitive behaviors. Those behaviors can look like many different things. Some people have a fear of germs and so compulsively wash their hands. Others flick light switches or jiggle door handles when entering or exiting a room. They might tap a railing a specific number of times or count their steps from the door to the car every single day.

These behaviors might seem silly to most of us, but for people living with OCD, they become all-consuming. These individuals feel like they have to continue this behavior or risk something terrible happening. They have an irrational fear of impending disaster and incorrectly connect their behaviors as the only thing protecting them from that disaster.

With exposure therapy, people with OCD are encouraged to let go of their behaviors, little by little, and learn to sit with the feelings of fear and anxiety that follow. So for example, if their behavior is washing their hands repetitively, a therapist might have them get their hands dirty and then not allow them to wash for several minutes. In doing so, the person learns to become comfortable with that feeling of anxiety and realizes that nothing terrible happened as a result of their dirty hands.

Once the person gains an understanding that their fears are unfounded and irrational, they are able to learn to feel at ease, even when those feelings of anxiety may arise. This ability to self-soothe is something that infants usually learn as a result of their earliest experiences.

For example, an infant has a need that is causing them discomfort or anxiety. Whether it's fear, hunger, pain, or some other physical, mental, or emotional need, the infant only has one tool at their disposal to have those needs met. They must alert a caregiver that they're in distress by crying and drawing attention to themselves.

When a caregiver responds to those cries for attention by meeting the infant's needs in a consistent way, the infant learns to expect that response. They will understand that their caregiver is reliable and trustworthy and will follow through when they need it most.

This provides a sense of security that the infant will carry with them through their development.

What happens as an infant develops into a child, and then a young adult, with a feeling of trust surrounding their caregivers is this – the child expects that their needs will be met eventually, even if it doesn't happen right away. They can live with the feeling that those unmet needs produce, feelings of anxiety and fear because they have a learned understanding that those feelings are only temporary and their caregiver will come through – like they always do.

This ability to self-soothe through uncomfortable feelings is a valuable life skill – and one that individuals with disorganized attachment styles often lack. As infants, they were not able to develop self-soothing techniques, because they were not granted the feeling of eventual safety and security from their caregivers. Their needs were not met when they cried out, at least not consistently, and so therefore they were left to sit with those feelings of fear and anxiety, and even learned to expect them.

Learning to Self-Soothe

When we self-soothe, we are using our coping mechanisms developed as young children and infants to help us regulate the emotions that are produced by fear. It always comes back to fear.

Trauma in early childhood has long-lasting repercussions and affects our whole selves as adults. We learn to suspect the world around us and the people we encounter and project our fears onto them even when it's not necessary.

Fear is an emotion that results from a self-preservation instinct. It's a deeply-seated, internal response formed in our subconscious brains – the part of our brains that is associated with the natural instinct to survive. Fear is our body's natural response to a situation that we deem to be unsafe, harmful, or detrimental to our physical well-being. It's a useful feeling that is inherent in human beings, as well as animals. It's designed to send our brain a signal to run when things seem unsafe – an instinct that likely served to keep us alive in the earliest days of the human species.

The problem arises when that fear response becomes embedded in our unconscious reactions, and we begin to attach it to people and things that are not actually threatening our well-being. Because of abuse, neglect, or traumatic experiences during infancy or childhood, our brains learn to expect harm more often than not - and the fear switch is turned on permanently. We lose the ability to rationalize when the fear is useful, and when it is unnecessary and actually stops serving us in any positive way.

Moving Out of Trauma

As adults, we have more resources at our disposal to keep ourselves safe from harm, both mentally and physically. As infants, we had no way to escape situations of abuse. As adults, we can move away from those situations, physically separating ourselves from the thing that has the potential to cause harm. Sort of like if you're crossing the street and you spot a vehicle barreling down on you, about to run you over. The survival instinct produces a fear response that triggers our brain to tell our body to move out of the way. And as fully grown, capable adults - we have the ability to do so.

An infant in the same situation doesn't have that choice, or the ability to remove themselves from harm. Any trauma and abuse they experience is a 24/7 experience that they are trapped within, by no fault of their own.

As adults, we have the ability to rationalize our situations and experiences, and mentally separate ourselves from people that may be causing harm to our emotional well-being. If we're in a toxic relationship or have a partner that belittles us and verbally accosts us, we can choose to remove ourselves from that situation. And we can rationalize the emotions that come with such a decision.

We may feel hurt, angry, or confused, but we have the cognizant ability to recognize those emotions for what they are and assign blame for them to the correct source. And we can move past those feelings without blaming ourselves for the outcome. We can decide if feelings of love are strong enough to justify working through issues in a relationship that is causing us harm, or if our personal happiness and well-being are too much at stake, then a break-up may make more sense for us personally.

An infant experiencing those same feelings is unable to understand them on that deep of a level. All they know is that a caregiver is causing them pain, sadness, fear, anger, and other feelings – and they have no way of understanding why that is happening. They may come to blame themselves for the response and the emotions they feel as a result. And those feelings of self-blame and low self-worth follow them throughout their development. They may even feel like they are deserving of the abuse and trauma they experience because they are unable to understand the reasoning behind the abuse any other way.

Carrying feelings of anger and fear with us into adulthood after experiencing abuse and trauma as infants is a common occurrence. And it can cause us to be hobbled as adults, stuck between the survival instinct that is permanently switched on and the desire to let go of that feeling of constant fear and uncertainty.

There is hope for trauma survivors – but achieving a sense of peace and security as adults can be challenging without facing those experiences that led us to where we are today. Some individuals may benefit from the help of a professional psychologist or counselor as they work through past traumas and try to heal. A professional has the skills and knowledge to help you uncover the root causes of your current emotional struggles and will be able to help you move through the recovery process at the right pace, healing hurts as you go along. It can be a long process and one that can cause emotional distress and even a physical reaction for some people. But trauma therapy has a high rate of success and offers the chance to find new ways to move forward in your life in a healthier way.

Trauma and Your Emotions

Experiencing trauma and abuse as a young infant can leave you with a host of emotions and triggers. Each of these emotions and feelings can get in the way of your attempts to develop meaningful relationships, by leading to self-sabotage syndrome. This is especially true for adults with disorganized attachment. Instead of processing these feelings leftover from negative childhood experiences, we find irrational ways to justify them, either projecting them onto ourselves or our partners.

Let's look at some of the common emotions and feelings that develop as a result of childhood abuse or trauma.

FEELINGS OF INADEQUACY

The suspicion that you're not good enough in some way, and the belief that your inadequacy will ultimately lead to your partner leaving you or cheating on you is a common emotion that develops from trauma. When we experience abuse as infants, we have no way to rationalize that behavior to ourselves, no way of explaining that the abuse is not our fault, but instead a shortcoming of the caregiver. We crave love and attention from our caregivers as infants, and when we don't receive it, we start to believe we must not be worthy of that love and attention. We develop feelings of inadequacy that can carry over into our adult relationships.

FEAR OF REJECTION

It's common for adults with a disorganized attachment style to hold false beliefs that people in their lives are ready to reject their love at every opportunity. This feeling stems from repeatedly suffering rejection from our caregivers as infants and children. We develop learned behavior because of the repeated push and pull we received from the adults in our lives, who may have shown love inconsistently, accepting our cries for affection in one instant, and rejecting them angrily in the next.

ANGER

It's not surprising that childhood trauma results in feelings of anger. For one thing, infants who suffer from abuse at the hands of their caregivers and grow up in that environment for a long time are certain to develop resentment toward those caregivers.

This feeling might not manifest itself while we are still infants, but it is certainly there.

Secondly, infants model their behavior after their environment and the behaviors of the adults around them. If a caregiver is constantly reacting in anger or displaying anger toward another person in the household, the infant will internalize that as normal behavior. Then, the adult they become will lash out in the same way.

Anger also surfaces as the result of fear, and other emotions that we cannot manage. Instead of facing those feelings that may cause discomfort, it's easier and safer for us to resort to anger. We feel more comfortable there and can gloss over the need to handle those other pesky emotions by focusing on the feeling that makes us feel the most powerful.

DEPRESSION

Trauma and depression often go hand-in-hand and can arise from feelings of hopelessness. Infants stuck in a cycle of abuse obviously had little hope for a way out. Now that those infants are adults and have carried their disorganized attachment style into their adult relationships, it can be easy to get stuck in that cycle of rotating emotions. It may feel like you will never be able to form a healthy bond with another person, and so you may feel like giving up hope altogether. Of course, all these feelings can lead to depression.

ANXIETY

Although disorganized attachment styles don't always develop the same way that anxious attachment styles do, there is still a good chance that feelings of anxiety will arise at some point. Anxiety is a response to our inability to feel secure in our environment, something adults with disorganized attachment likely experienced as infants.

Like most emotions, it stems from a place of fear. The fear of the unknown, and our inability to expect a consistent response from those around us. We always feel as if things are teetering on a precipice and one wrong move will spell disaster.

Finding Ways to Cope

The key to working through the powerful emotions that come with a disorganized attachment style and result from abuse and trauma experiences from childhood is to acknowledge a few truths to ourselves.

TRUTH #1 – YOU ARE SAFE RIGHT NOW.

Fear is the driving force behind most actions and emotions associated with trauma. There is an underlying expectation of pain – and that expectation leads to a constant state of heightened awareness and fear.

When you start to notice those recognizable emotions associated with fear, take a moment to stop and remind yourself that you aren't in any danger at this very moment. Remind yourself as many times as necessary, until you start to feel the fear and anxiety abate a little bit.

TRUTH #2 – YOU ARE NOT THE CHILD YOU ONCE WERE.

Feelings left over after trauma and abuse are very real – and are the result of very real experiences. They are valid responses to the experiences that you lived through.

However, it's important to remember that those scenarios that existed once upon a time are no longer your reality.

You are not an infant, or a small child, at the mercy of the actions of others. You are a fully-capable, strong, developed adult human, with physical and mental capabilities that you didn't possess all those years ago. Remind yourself of that when feelings of fear start to creep in.

TRUTH #3 - YOU CAN RECOVER, AND YOU ARE WORTH IT.

Make this your mantra - and whenever you start to feel like giving up, repeat it to yourself. Childhood abuse and trauma are terrible, debilitating experiences that forever change the trajectory of a life. But that doesn't mean you can't walk a different road and move forward.

You deserve to feel safe, and you deserve to enjoy healthy relationships with your friends, family members, and romantic partners. There doesn't need to be a rope tying you to your past. Looking back is one thing, but failing to look forward is sure to keep you stuck in one spot. Remember: you can recover, and you are worth it.

Tips for Conquering Fear

When those feelings of fear become recognizable, tangible things in your everyday life, then, it's time to take action. The following tips are designed to help you be mindful of your current situation and surroundings and they will help you slowly reprogram your brain and your behavior from the fear state into something more manageable.

It won't happen overnight, and it will take lots of practice. There will be times when even these interventions don't seem to calm your emotions. But keep at it and keep working to overcome those fears that are crippling your development and hindering your ability to be a functional, balanced, and peaceful human being.

1. TAKE A MOMENT

Fear is a feeling that can seem overwhelming. Extreme fear and anxiety can manifest in physical ways – a pounding heart, a racing pulse, trembling or tremors, shortness of breath, and cold or hot sweats.

When you start to notice the fear cycle starting up, it's important to take a moment and cut the cord. There is a connection between your fear and your subconscious. Taking a moment to separate yourself from that emotion can reset your inner balance and stop the cycle in its tracks.

Try to distract yourself by doing an activity you truly enjoy. Take a walk outside. Play with a favorite pet. Have a hot cup of tea or enjoy a bubble bath. Listen to soothing music. Find any activity that you enjoy and that results in positive emotions and feelings, and focus on that activity until you start to feel calmer and more at ease.

2. DEEP BREATHING

Deep breathing techniques can help stop the body's physical reaction to fear. It's sort of like holding your breath when you have hiccups. The idea is to break the cycle that is building to an inevitable end of you feeling unworthy and your fear winning the day. Don't let it happen.

You may not have control of everything in your life. Nobody does. But one thing you can control is your own breathing. Even when your heart is racing and your palms are sweating, remember that you are in control of your physical capacity.

Take a series of slow, deep breaths - in through the nose and out through the mouth. Make sure you maintain a breathing rhythm that is comfortable for you. As you breathe through the fear and panic, your whole being will begin to get used to the feeling of sitting inside the emotions. Nothing bad is going to happen as a result of those emotions - they're just emotions, and you can breathe through them to live another moment.

3. BE MINDFUL OF YOUR SURROUNDINGS

One of the best ways to reset our fear cycles is to simply take a look around. Notice where you are in time and space at this very moment. In doing so, it becomes easier to understand and truly believe that you are safe at this moment, and the feelings of fear will slowly abate over time.

If you can find a moment to step outside, do so. Look up at the sky. Notice the clouds floating by. See the trees swaying their branches in the wind. Listen to the sounds of nature around you. Breathe in the oxygen and feel the air on your skin.

Once you have taken a moment to really become mindful of your surroundings, ask yourself this question: Where is the danger? The answer is likely to be that there isn't any. The only place you can be right now is where you already are, and if there is no immediate threat to your physical well-being in your present environment, then that fear you're feeling is unwarranted and not necessary for your survival. Let it go.

4. VISUALIZATION

Visualization techniques can be very useful for people struggling with fear emotions. It allows your brain, which is caught in that never-ending cycle of fear and anxiety, to immerse itself in a different emotion – one with positive feelings attached to it.

Visualization takes practice, but once you have tried it a couple of times, I guarantee you will find a sense of relief afterward.

To try visualization, close your eyes and imagine yourself in a place of peace and tranquility. This can be a place you know well, somewhere you have visited in the past, or a place generated entirely from your imagination. The most important thing is that it needs to be a place that stimulates positive emotions and feelings of peace within you.

Get as detailed with your visualization as your mind will allow you to. Look around and notice details about the location. Is it nighttime, or is the sun shining? Is it warm there, or cool like Autumn? Is there snow on the ground, or are there flowers in bloom?

If your mind starts to wander from your visualization back into reality, that's okay. Don't chide yourself for it – simply pick up where you left off. Acknowledge your reality and then put yourself right back into your happy place.

5. FACE YOUR FEARS

One of the best ways to overcome our fears is to face them. If your fear is something tangible and available in your current reality, like a fear of spiders or being afraid to use the elevator, for example, then facing your fear is pretty easy. All you have to do is find some spiders or take a ride on that elevator!

However, when your fear is irrational and is an effect of abuse and trauma suffered in your early days of development, facing your fear might become more difficult. Unless you're willing to face your abuser, if they're still around, and experience the fear of being in proximity to them.

Many trauma and abuse survivors decide to cut ties with their abusers. Others may choose not to. Loyalty to family and loved ones can keep them bound to the very person who caused so much hurt and pain in the first place. Deciding how to approach situations like this is very personal, and nobody can tell you what the right decision is for you, except for you. It's a decision and a course of action that often involves the help of a professional counselor to navigate.

If facing your abuser is not something you feel comfortable doing, there's no shame in that decision. You are your own person now, and you owe nothing to anybody who has caused you pain, whether intentionally or not. Forgiving them might make some people feel better able to move on. And some people may feel like they can never forgive. That's okay too.

Another way to face your fears is by determining how you are transposing them onto something else. Many adults with disorganized attachments project their fears onto people close to them. That's where the feelings of jealousy and anger come from, and it can lead to mistrust. Examine those feelings when they arise, acknowledge the reasons that they are irrational and unjustified, and then keep moving. Congratulations, you have faced your fears!

6. TALK THERAPY

One of the biggest benefits of visiting a professional therapist or counselor is having someone to talk to. Verbalizing your experiences can help you move past them and having someone who truly empathizes with your feelings can help you feel like someone cares.

You could also confide in a close friend, family member, or even your romantic partner. Explain to them that you just need someone to listen for a minute or two and that you would appreciate their attention.

If you don't have access to anyone you feel comfortable talking with, there are online resources that can connect you with mental health professionals, including pairing you with someone willing to listen to your concerns and respond with empathy.

Ready to Move Forward?

Dealing with childhood trauma and the emotions that come along for the ride into adulthood is a complicated process. There might never come a day of realization as you see in the movies - where you wake up and suddenly realize you're over it and ready to move on. But healing can happen when you take the time for yourself.

Healing from trauma is all about acknowledging that the trauma occurred, recognizing the effect it has had on your development, and then understanding that it's not your fault.

Once you have accepted these truths, you will be better able to manage your emotions, understand your responses, and learn to self-soothe through moments of fear and anxiety. After conquering that skill, you can focus on making better decisions and realizing that you are in control of your own actions.

You deserved better from the adults around you, and you deserve love, compassion, and empathy from others now, just as you did back then. You are not that little child anymore and you don't have to allow your past experiences to dictate your present situation.

There is a way out of the feelings left over from past abuse and trauma experiences. Nothing is set in stone and our development as human beings continues throughout our lives. You can change going forward.

You have the power to heal. And you deserve it. Now, let's move on to learn other ways to cope with your emotions, like learning what triggers them in the first place.

Chapter 4 – The Cause-and-Effect Theory

Learning what triggers people with disorganized attachment and what to do when these triggers occur.

The cause-and-effect theory can be explained with a short story about a friend of mine. For the sake of the story, we will call her Rose.

Rose's Story

I met Rose when I was in my early twenties. We were introduced through a mutual friend. In just a few short weeks, Rose and I were fast friends, sharing secrets and causing more trouble than we probably deserved to get away with. But hey, we were young!

Rose was married at a very young age and had her first child shortly after. She married her high school sweetheart, the only serious relationship she had ever experienced at that time. Within months of their wedding, her husband took a job overseas. Like, way overseas. And

Rose, with an ailing father to care for and a brand-new baby, was left alone.

Rose's mother had passed away a few years prior to her marriage, when she was just a teenager - the result of a brain tumor. Rose didn't speak of her mother. She never shared that particular secret with me, or anyone else I was aware of. The only reason I even knew her mother had passed was because she had a tattoo in remembrance of her, with her mother's birthday and the year of her death.

Now, I don't know what life was like for Rose as a child. I don't know enough about her situation to say for certain that she had a disorganized attachment, but what I do know is that she definitely exhibited signs of insecure attachment.

When Rose's mother passed away, Rose was left without a familial figure that she obviously felt love and affection for. Losing a parent unexpectedly at such a young, pivotal age can be a tough burden to bear. And there was Rose, left alone without her mother.

When Rose's husband left to take a job overseas, something he believed was best for his family at the time (or so he said), Rose was left alone again. The fact that her husband claimed to have her best interests in mind didn't numb the pain of months and months, and eventually three whole years with a few visits mixed in, of feeling abandoned by someone she trusted.

So, we clearly see the cause in this scenario – an unstable upbringing and a series of perceived abandonments. Now let's examine the effect.

Rose was a party animal, and I was drawn to her effusive personality. She seemed to ooze self-confidence, comfortable walking into a room full of strangers and making friends with every single one of them effortlessly. Shy as I was at a young age, I was drawn to her confidence and followed behind her on a string of ill-advised adventures.

Our friendship didn't last very long, however, because it became clear to me very quickly that Rose's apparent happy-go-lucky behavior was a cover for a broken, hurt, and insecure person. She would cycle from all the way up to all the way down; happy and engaging one evening and withdrawn and sulky the next morning.

Not only that, but Rose was purposefully mean. I didn't see it right away, because she was always nice to me (lucky me). But she had no such loyalty to newly met friends or strangers. She would act out in strange ways, doing or saying things clearly designed to hurt or embarrass someone else. And she seemed to enjoy the way those actions made her feel, like a power play that proved she had more worth than someone else.

And then came the infidelity. I don't fault Rose for her decisions, and I certainly don't judge her actions. And as coincidence would have it, her husband was enjoying a few of his own flings while he was far across the ocean. But these encounters that Rose constantly chased were strange to me because they were clearly a cry for attention – from anyone who would willingly give it to her. And because she kept these interactions informal, never expressing love for her conquests, she never opened herself up to the possibility of being left alone again. As a matter of fact, more often than not, it was Rose who did the leaving.

The Cause and Effect Dynamic in Action

So, are Rose's uneven and confusing behaviors a direct result of her early experiences in life? Is there a cause and effect between being abandoned and acting impulsively in return, almost in a clear effort to elicit a reaction from her far-away husband? Clearly, there is a cause-and-effect dynamic at work here.

Disorganized attachment is a perfect example of the cause-and-effect theory at work.

The infant suffers from abuse, neglect, and trauma – this is the cause of disorganized attachment.

The adult has trouble forming relationships, difficulty managing extreme highs and lows, and often finds themselves self-sabotaging relationships that otherwise seem healthy and promising – this is the effect.

To dig even further back into the cause and effect, consider the neglectful caregiver themselves. This is not an effort to excuse abuse and neglect, of course. However, it can be beneficial for your own personal healing to understand how far-reaching cause and effect can be.

The neglectful, abusive caregiver was once an infant as well. That infant lived through unique experiences and situations and had caregivers of their own. And guess what? Those caregivers had a direct effect on how that infant developed - causing and affecting the behaviors that resulted in your own personal abuse and trauma. Look even further back into the family tree, and it is likely that the cycle of neglect and abuse followed by more neglect and abuse goes back a long way.

Breaking the cycle of abuse isn't always easy, and it takes self-awareness on the part of the abuser. And not every abuse survivor will wind up as an abuser themselves. However, it's very likely that those with the tendency to abuse, or the inability to be consistent, successful caregivers, lacked something in their own upbringing that caused them to end up the way they were as adults.

Cause and effect are what lead to the development of a disorganized attachment style - and it doesn't end there. Because cause and effect is also an explanation for an individual's reactions when dealing with a disorganized attachment. There will be situations and environments, and even people, that trigger a fear response in those individuals, even when there is nothing tangible to fear. This trigger is a cause and effect in and of itself.

Everything in life has a cause - and every cause has a resulting effect.

What is a Trigger?

Think of it like this: a trigger is a mechanism on a gun that, when pulled, causes the gun to fire. It causes an explosion of gunpowder that propels a bullet toward a target and causes substantial damage in the process.

In the realm of behavioral health, a trigger is something that causes a specific response from someone, based on past experiences and learned behavior. To be "triggered" has actually become a slang phrase used by the younger generation. It is often used to explain why someone reacts with anger or strong emotions in response to something else. The "something else" is the "trigger" that causes a person to feel a certain way.

Triggers don't always have to lead to anger. On the contrary, every strong emotion can have a trigger, even positive ones. A smiling child might trigger you to feel happy and smile yourself. A visit from a friend who you haven't seen in a long time might trigger feelings of nostalgia. And a sad movie ending might trigger emotions like sadness.

These triggers are powerful and are not damaging to our well-being in any sustainable way.

But for adults living with a disorganized attachment, the term trigger can take us to a scary, fear-filled place. And those triggers could also cause behaviors that we later regret and cause us to take actions that we later wish we could take back - kind of how my friend Rose would act out because of strong emotions she didn't know how to handle, and then feel entirely different about her choices the very next day.

Learning to understand where your triggers come from and how they developed in response to certain traumatic childhood experiences is the first step to being able to weather the feelings they create within us. For trauma and abuse survivors, these triggers don't just make us feel uncomfortable. They can literally cause us to regress back to how we felt as children in those moments of fear and pain. In an instant, you can feel almost transported back in time, stuck in scary, familiar situations we can't escape.

Once you have identified those things that trigger you, it can be easier to avoid them. Or if you find yourself unable to avoid a specific trigger, you can focus instead on working through the emotions, feelings, and memories that arise inside of you when you're confronted with that trigger. You can learn to acknowledge your feelings and then choose to move past them, without becoming stuck inside memories of traumatic events that are no longer occurring, and therefore no longer a threat.

It can be helpful to identify certain situations that can act as triggers for individuals living with disorganized attachment. Below are a few examples of the most common triggers and some practical advice on how to move through these triggers in the healthiest way possible.

FEELINGS OF REJECTION

If you have a disorganized attachment style then you likely feel as if your partner is plotting to leave you, either intermittently or all of the time. This feeling can stem from similar experiences of rejection experienced as an infant or during early childhood. You come to expect rejection because you are accustomed to it, and have an unfounded belief that everyone, eventually, will find a reason to reject you.

Feelings of rejection are hard to combat. For a person living with disorganized attachment, even the smallest and most unintentional actions can leave us feeling vulnerable to abandonment. Maybe your partner doesn't answer the phone on the first ring or fails to return your phone calls right away. Maybe your partner spends a few extra hours at work in the evening or even comes home a few minutes late because they are stuck in traffic. Maybe your partner is extra tired one evening and doesn't feel like going out for dinner.

These innocuous actions are likely not actual signs of impending rejection from your partner, but if you struggle with disorganized attachment then your mind may make an incorrect correlation between those actions and the likelihood of your partner leaving you.

EMOTIONAL INTIMACY

Emotional intimacy is a cornerstone of a healthy relationship and can be one of the best parts of creating a real connection with another person. But for the individual living with disorganized attachment, those moments of emotional connection can actually feel scary. You have learned that being emotionally available to another person leaves you wide open for hurt and pain and being put in a similar situation as an adult will likely feel the same way.

A person living with a disorganized attachment will crave emotional intimacy, whether with a romantic partner, a close friend, or a family member. But truly opening up to another person feels like a dangerous place. When those feelings of openness and emotion start to get too close to your protective barriers, the fight or flight instinct will set in and cause you to push away from the very thing you want. It can also cause you to feel triggered, bringing back memories of fear and vulnerability that feel uncomfortable and unsustainable.

PHYSICAL INTIMACY OR TOUCH

Both true physical intimacy and touch can be triggers for someone with a disorganized attachment, especially if that person experienced physical or sexual violence in the past. These types of abuse are commonly found in the early developmental years of those who end up with a disorganized attachment. Experiencing this type of abuse can be truly damaging and traumatic for anyone and obviously creates a long-lasting effect that carries over into adulthood.

A simple touch at the wrong moment or in the wrong place can trigger memories of past trauma and abuse. And being physically intimate with a romantic partner certainly has the potential to bring negative memories and connotations. These triggers can be especially hard to deal with and can leave people feeling both mentally and physically unable to connect with another person. And that's a terrible feeling.

Human beings need physical touch – we crave it with our subconscious mind. Infants who are denied physical touch often end up completely unsocialized and unable to develop past a certain age mentally. And infants who are exposed to angry touch, the kind of touch that causes pain and fear, will end up expecting that same kind of touch even decades later from their partners.

FEELINGS OF UNCERTAINTY

Disorganized attachment develops when an infant or child often feels uncertain regarding the expected reactions from their caregivers. They never know if their cries for attention and care will be rewarded with love and affection, or anger, pain, and fear – or even with no reaction at all. This environment puts them in a place where they never know what to expect, and because of that, they develop into adults who constantly feel like they are standing on unstable ground.

Triggers for these emotions can come from a lot of different sources. Being put in situations that feel unsafe or uncomfortable might trigger feelings of fear. Receiving uneven responses from those people we are trying to build relationships with can make the person with disorganized attachment feel those ingrained emotions they associate with uncertainty.

FEELINGS OF SUSPICION

If you have a disorganized attachment, those previous feelings of uncertainty can sometimes trigger other emotions of their own. These emotions might be formed in reaction to interactions with those around you, or they might stem from internal feelings of low self-worth and feeling as if you actually deserve abandonment and rejection.

Feelings of suspicion are common among people with disorganized attachment, and they can trigger a total fear state in response. Often, that fear manifests itself in reactions of jealousy and anger, causing you to lash out at the source of that suspicion, even if it's unwarranted and unjustified.

TRAUMA ASSOCIATIONS

Individuals who live through traumatic upbringings will often hold onto subconscious associations to those moments. Everyone will likely experience different trauma associations because everyone's trauma probably looked very different in detail.

For example, if you suffered abuse at the hands of a caregiver who was often inebriated and smelled of alcohol, then smelling alcohol on someone you encountered as an adult could trigger you back into that state of fear. If you had a caregiver who restrained you or locked you in a room for lengthy periods, then feeling trapped or unable to move might be a trigger. If you had a caregiver who often yelled and screamed at you as an infant, then loud voices and noisy places might be a trigger.

How to Deal with Troublesome Triggers

As I mentioned before, triggers for people who suffered from abuse or neglect as infants are more than inconvenient. People suffering from a disorganized attachment can be downright crippling, leading us to feel emotionally stunted and unable to move past the feelings they bring out in us. Certain triggers can lead to what feels like a complete emotional breakdown and result in those emotions manifesting in full-bodied physical symptoms.

But there are ways to feel better and be able to function, even when those triggers cause us to feel like it's impossible. For those people experiencing the fear and strong emotions brought on by a trigger, it can be easy to get stuck in those emotions. It can sometimes be easier to simply shut down altogether – or lash out at those around you.

For those on the outside, being witness to an emotional breakdown from a partner with disorganized attachment can be scary and overwhelming. You might not understand the emotions your partner is experiencing and be unaware of what specifically triggered them in the first place. The resulting whirlwind can make you feel completely out of control, eager to step in and say or do something that will make your partner feel better, and hesitant to do anything that will make the situation worse.

Let's go over some tips on how to avoid those triggers you already know about, and how to move through the storm of emotions you may feel after experiencing an emotional trigger.

If you're the one personally struggling with a disorganized attachment, getting stuck in the emotions that arise after a trauma trigger arises can be scary and stressful. The most important thing you can do to start to feel better is to remind yourself that you are safe right now. Try to slow your breathing, taking deep breaths in through your nose and out through your mouth. Be cognizant of your current surroundings and reassert yourself into the present moment.

Triggers have such a powerful effect on our mental state because they are subconsciously tied to past trauma, and that trauma can exert a powerful hold over our current state of being. Certain triggers can transport us right back to a time when we were unsafe and at risk. Fight the pull of the past and remind yourself where you are right now - and you will slowly break the hold that those past memories have on you. And never, ever blame yourself for feeling the way you do. Trauma was something that was done to you, not something you did to yourself - and the reactions you carry with you into adulthood are the direct result of that trauma. There's no shame in feeling those strong emotions, and no reason to chide yourself for breaking down from time to time. The important thing is not to get stuck there, but rather find ways to get up and brush yourself back off so you can continue enjoying your life.

If your trigger is something that can be avoided, then it might be beneficial to limit your exposure to that thing until you have better control over your physical and emotional responses. For example, if you're triggered by the smell of alcohol on someone's breath then try to avoid situations where you are surrounded by people who are drinking alcohol. If you're triggered by loud voices, explain that to your partner or other people in your life so they can understand how it makes you feel. If your friends, family, and partners can clearly understand what triggers you and why they can take steps themselves to avoid putting you in situations where you might feel fearful or uncomfortable.

If your partner is the one suffering from a disorganized attachment and finds themselves easily triggered by certain situations, then it can be difficult to know exactly how you should respond. The most important thing to remember is that the emotional outbursts or physical manifestations of emotions that your partner is experiencing are out of their control. It's an automatic, unconscious response to the past abuse and neglect that was done to them by someone else. These people are likely not being purposefully difficult, and instead, find themselves stuck in a loop of fear and reaction.

Here are some tips on how to handle a negative response to trauma triggers in a partner, friend, or loved one.

- Give them space to experience their emotions without fear of ridicule or anger in response.

- Don't tell them to "snap out of it," or "get over it."

- Speak in a calm voice and keep your body language non-confrontational

- Don't try to comfort them physically until they let you know that's what they need.

- Ask them how you can help.

- Remind them that they are in a safe place.

- Give them your complete attention and focus.

- Explain that you are there for them and that they can lean on you for support if they need it.

- Ask them to explain how they're feeling in the moment, but don't push if they're not ready to share.

- Express empathy and compassion for their situation and explain that the emotions they are experiencing are a normal reaction to their past experiences.

- Try to refocus their attention on the present.

- Don't force the situation to switch from distressing to happy. When your partner is ready to move past their emotions and recenter on the present, they will let you know.

- Reinforce the idea that an emotional breakdown is not the end of the world, or the end of your relationship together. Let them know you will still be around, no matter how many times a trigger sends them spiraling into strong emotions.

- Ask your partner if there is something you have said or done that contributed to them feeling the way they do and offer to find constructive ways to avoid repeating those situations in the future.

Surviving Triggers – and Moving Beyond

The biggest part of surviving through the emotional baggage that is directly attached to certain triggers is understanding why those triggers cause us to feel the way we do. When we can understand how a certain trigger formed in our subconscious and assign our emotional and physical reactions to that trigger to their proper source – which is trauma, abuse, or neglect suffered during our earliest years – then it's easier to understand that we are in no real danger in the present.

Reasserting your control over your emotions, responses, reactions, and feelings is a powerful step toward recovery from a disorganized attachment. These situations can make you feel completely out of control and at the mercy of your subconscious reactions, but it doesn't have to be that way. It will take practice and time, and it won't be easy every step of the way. But with a better understanding of ourselves and the support of friends, family, and loved ones, we can move safely past trauma triggers without always needing to get caught up in the fallout.

Chapter 5 – The Surprising Power of Communication

How the power of communication is the glue that holds relationships together.

We have already covered the definition of disorganized attachment and described how it develops. We have spoken about how the disorganized attached person struggles to form close bonds with the people in their lives, because the feeling of intimacy and openness, for them, go hand in hand with fear and vulnerability.

We covered the emotions that arise when an individual with disorganized attachment starts to feel like a relationship is getting too close to their inner barriers, becoming more of a threat than seems possible to endure. Or, when that person is triggered by some emotion, sensation, or situation that brings back memories of the terrible abuse and trauma they lived through as infants or children.

The aim of this book is to help you, as an individual with a disorganized attachment, or you, as the partner of someone who is living with a disorganized attachment, to find practical ways to move past the trauma and change the behaviors that are stopping you from finding a truly healthy relationship.

So, now it's time to dive into one of the most useful and constructive tools that we, as human beings, have at our disposal – the power of language and communication.

It is said that the power to form detailed and descriptive language is one of the characteristics that set us apart from the rest of the animal kingdom. Our gift of speaking our feelings into existence, sharing those feelings with each other, and therefore gaining a better understanding of each other is unique among humans.

And yet, even animals develop ways to communicate with each other – albeit not with words. They do, however, use a combination of sounds and vocal patterns that are designed to communicate messages to other animals around them; messages of warning, messages to communicate with their young, and messages to alert others of danger. For animals, this skill is inherent. It's a part of their natural instincts used to keep them safe and alive.

Humans have taken that inherent skill and expanded on it, using our enhanced ability to reason to build an entire language. We use the skill of communication in much the same way that animals do – to communicate a need, warn others of danger, and teach and protect our offspring. But thanks to the evolution of our species, we can do much more with it than just that.

Communication – The Basis of Relationships

Relationships of any kind rely on communication. A relationship that lacks communication is likely to be one where misunderstandings and assumptions cloud reality, causing distress and disharmony between the two people. Even poor communication can be a hindrance rather than a benefit, causing people to say things they don't mean, overreact to their partner's words or actions, and make bad decisions in regard to their own responses.

Remember that the disorganized attacher lives in a fluctuating state of emotions; at one time anxious and hyper-emotional and at other times avoidant, angry, and cold. What results is someone who has a hard time understanding their own emotions from one moment to the next, and an even harder time communicating those feelings to someone else.

In a healthy relationship, two partners use communication in several ways.

1. To help the other person better understand how they are feeling

2. To show the other person affection

3. To demonstrate a particular need

4. To work through problems and find solutions

5. To negotiate differences of opinion and find a middle ground

These are some of the basics of communication as it works in relationships. Communication in a healthy relationship is open and trusting. One partner does not fear ridicule, rejection, or anger from the other partner as a result of their sharing their feelings. This creates an even ground, where nobody is above or below anyone else. Both partners have the ability to speak openly when something is bothering them, when they feel hurt or confused by something, or when they have a particular need that they would like fulfilled.

Communication in a healthy relationship also manifests itself as a love language, even in cases where the relationship is not a romantic one. People are able to communicate feelings of love and affection for another person without the expectation of fear or rejection in return. This is especially true in relationships where trust has already been established and there is a preexisting sense of closeness between the two people.

For example, two people who are best friends and have been for years and years will often express love for each other. It's not romantic love – it exists in a more platonic way. But it is certainly there. It's a bond that has been formed over time as two people share experiences and open up to each other about their feelings - their hopes and dreams, their fears, and feelings of inadequacy.

And in a healthy relationship, that type of communication can be done without feeling unsafe. As a matter of fact, opening up to a close friend, family member, or romantic partner can actually make us feel safer, loved, and protected -because we have an understanding that the other person loves us in return, only wants the best for us in everything, and will listen openly and respectfully without judgment.

When disorganized attachment enters the mix, suddenly communication becomes more difficult. If you are navigating relationships with a disorganized attachment style, then open communication with someone else can make you feel vulnerable and at risk of hurt. Openly communicating with someone else puts you in a place where there is an expectation that you reveal all of your secrets, bare your soul, and do so without any immediate defense of your emotional well-being. When put that way, doesn't it sound kind of scary?

If your ingrained response to those feelings of vulnerability and defenselessness is to move into an automatic fear state, then being expected to openly communicate can certainly be scary. And as a result, the individual with a disorganized attachment style will react unexpectedly and in confusing ways. It's the see-saw effect in action.

In one breath they may express feelings of love and wanting to be close to someone else, and in the next breath, they are giving into that fear response and lashing out as the result. The individual can internalize that fear of rejection and hurt and shut down or they inadvertently transpose those feelings of uncertainty onto their partners, finding any reason to push them away and revert once again to a place they consider safe.

How to Communicate with Disorganized Attachment

There are practical steps you can take to improve your personal communication skills if you are existing in a state of disorganized attachment. And it's important that you recognize your role in the conversation because communication is a two-way street. Both partners must learn to openly communicate their feelings in a healthy, non-confrontational way if any positive outcome is expected at the end. Failure to face these barriers to your communication with other people is certain to create further distrust on behalf of both people.

Let's examine some tools you can use to better communicate your feelings if you have a disorganized attachment style.

THINK BEFORE YOU SPEAK

Internal associations left over from childhood can lead you to incorrectly react to certain situations. As soon as you start feeling vulnerable, there can be the temptation to react with extreme emotions, and you may not even realize it's happening right away. But remember that those strong emotional reactions are the result of learned behavior resulting from negative childhood experiences.

It's important that you take a moment and examine your motivations when interacting with someone else because it's hard to take back words once they are spoken. If your partner or loved one is aware of your attachment issues and willing to work through them, then that might benefit you in the long run. Your partner may be more forgiving when you act out with a display of extreme emotions or shut down entirely. But if you're looking to build a new relationship with someone and are just in the process of getting to know another person, you likely won't have that space to make mistakes, at least not too many times. Saying hurtful things or reacting with fear and jealousy is a turn-off for many people, no matter if your intentions are conscious or unconscious.

HOLD OFF ON BIG DECISIONS

In order for communication between two people to work there needs to be enough time given to work thorough issues. And if you have a disorganized attachment style, it can be all too easy to react by running as far and fast as you can. Engaging in open communication with another person can certainly be a trauma trigger and is likely to bring on feelings of vulnerability and fear. And what do you think we have we learned about people who have a disorganized attachment style when they are faced with situations that cause them discomfort or fear? They run!

Communication is hard and takes practice, especially when it involves serious issues that arise in relationships. No relationship will ever be 100% harmonious all of the time. There are going to be occasions when you disagree with your partner. Sometimes those disagreements are small and seemingly unimportant, like what to have for breakfast. And other times, those disagreements can be in regard to much more important issues with lasting repercussions.

The important thing to remember when you are engaging in conversation is to give yourself time to think things through. If the conversation starts to feel too heavy or triggering, it's okay to step away for a moment, or even for the rest of the day. But you must try to openly communicate your need to detach from the conversation with your partner so they don't feel as if you're simply giving up on them. Let them know you need some time to decompress and reset your emotions before continuing. And then allow yourself time to do just that without making rash decisions like ending the relationship for good because you feel unsafe at the moment.

USE "I" STATEMENTS TO EXPRESS YOURSELF

Communication is a skill that takes practice, even for those with the healthiest and most open relationships. If you have a disorganized attachment style, you might find yourself projecting your emotions onto your partner without realizing it. Instead of expressing how you are personally feeling, you transpose those emotions onto your partner and wind up making the conversation completely about their actions instead of your feelings. This is guaranteed to leave your partner feeling attacked and often unjustly so.

When engaged in a conversation with a partner, practice expressing your feelings using "I" statements. In doing so, you will gain a better understanding of exactly what is causing you to feel the way you do. Starting your sentence by assigning responsibility for your feelings to yourself, instead of to your partner, will provide you with a better perspective of where those feelings come from. Let's look at this theory in practice.

Don't say: *"You're going to cheat on me."*

Instead, say: *"I worry sometimes that you're going to cheat on me."*

Don't say: *"You don't love me enough, that's why you don't return my phone calls right away."*

Instead, say: *"I worry that you don't love me when you don't return my phone calls right away."*

Notice how the first statements include assumptions, that as far as we know right now, are unfounded. It's easy to see the difference phrasing can make when examining the above statements. Simply putting the "I" at the beginning of the sentence, allows you to easily identify those statements that might be unfounded. For example, when you say, *"You're going to cheat on me,"* it leaves the reason for those feelings out of the equation. Changing the sentence to *"I worry that you're going to cheat on me,"* forces you to examine the reasons behind those feelings, and it changes the sentence from being an accusation against your partner to a chance to work through your own fear-based emotions.

For example, if your statement is about a fear of your partner cheating on you, then it's only logical to ask yourself why you feel that way. Is your partner acting suspiciously? Have you caught your partner in a lie? Have you any actual reason at all to suspect your partner of cheating? Or is there an internalized feeling of low self-worth and not being good enough that is causing you to expect a partner to cheat on you? If the answer is that there is no real reason to suspect your partner of what you are accusing them of, then the issue likely stems from your disorganized attachment. You are expecting catastrophic events when there is no reason to.

Let's examine the second sentence. When you say, *"You don't love me enough,"* as the reason why your partner doesn't return your phone calls right away, you are projecting your internal fears onto them as an explanation for their actions. In proper, give-and-take communication it would make more sense to ask your partner outright why they don't return your phone calls right away and then explain how that makes you feel.

The correct way to express that question, by saying, "*I worry that you don't love me when you don't return my phone calls right away,*" does two things. First, it allows your partner to explain why they didn't return your phone calls right away. Maybe, just maybe, there is a reasonable explanation for their actions that you haven't considered.

And secondly, it allows you to express how their actions make you feel without accusing them of not loving you. Saying something makes you feel a certain way doesn't automatically equate to that feeling being true. Expressing your emotions in this way also allows your partner to clearly understand how their actions are impacting your well-being. An open and supportive partner might respond by explaining that they didn't know how you felt when they didn't return your calls right away and then offer to make a greater effort to do so if it's something that bothers you so much.

How to Communicate with a Hot and Cold Partner

If you are the partner of someone living with a disorganized attachment style, then communication will take some extra effort on your part. If that's something you are willing to offer your partner, and if you're reading this book then I assume it is, then you have a good chance of being exactly the kind of person your partner needs in their life to help them receive what they need most from a relationship, which is to feel safe.

So how exactly should you respond to a partner who has a disorganized attachment and reacts unpredictably at times? How can you effectively communicate with someone who sends mixed signals and seems to never say what they're actually feeling? The goal is to deconstruct the mixed signals your partner is sending and strip away their defenses so that both of you can recognize and deal with the true emotions that are driving their response, which is fear.

Now stripping away your partner's defenses might sound confrontational. And if done incorrectly, it certainly will feel that way to them. Nobody likes being put on the spot or having fingers pointed at them. And if the goal is to build a stronger communication bond, then that tactic will backfire anyhow, causing your partner to feel even more unsafe and insecure.

Instead, this deconstructing needs to be done subtly, slowly, and with empathy. It can't come from a place of anger or hurt on your part, even when your partner is saying things designed to be hurtful. Remember that the intentions of those reactions are simply to give them an excuse to push you away so they can feel safe again.

Here are some tips for building open and effective communication with a partner with a disorganized attachment style.

- Let your partner know you're there for them.

- Express empathy and compassion for how they are feeling.

- Be ready to listen when your partner is ready to talk.

- Don't accuse or point fingers when your partner responds irrationally.

- Speak in a calm voice and remain non-confrontational.

- If a partner makes unfounded accusations, calmly point out that those reactions are unjustified.

- Ask your partner what they need to feel safe.

- Share your own feelings and emotions with your partner to show them that a relationship can be a safe place.

- Give your partner the time and space to feel safe communicating with you.

- Help your partner work through strong emotions by offering them a safe space to talk, every single time.

Communication in any relationship takes work, practice, and even give-and-take between both people. The trouble with individuals with disorganized attachment is that they often say or do things they don't really mean or they don't completely understand their motivations in doing so. Approaching communication with these people must be done strategically and with the understanding that they truly want to build a safe and trusting relationship, even when they are expressing something very different. Offer a truly safe place for your partner to communicate. Show them that being vulnerable doesn't automatically result in pain and hurt, and eventually, that partner will start to build trust in that fact.

Communication Pitfalls

Even the most well-adjusted relationships require hard work and commitment. And that includes a commitment to building an open and effective communication style that accounts for both partners' emotional needs.

It might sound difficult, and at times it can be. But by remaining empathetic to your partner's feelings, you can work together on the skill and get better at it over time. Here are a few common pitfalls that couples fall into when attempting to communicate with each other.

Resulting to insults - Communication is often used when partners need to resolve serious disagreements or disputes. This can result in strong emotions on both sides, and it doesn't take long for those emotions to manifest themselves through jabs and insults. Trading insults is a scenario that can spiral out of control. One partner says something hurtful, and the other partner retaliates by saying something hurtful in response.

Don't let strong emotions get the better of you when communicating. Take some deep breaths, refocus on your intentions, and respond with empathy and understanding. When all else fails, take a break and come back to the conversation when both partners have cooled down.

The silent treatment - Individuals with disorganized attachment tend to fear intimacy, both physical and emotional. Open communication is likely to leave them feeling vulnerable and might result in them completely closing off. Whether they do it out of fear or because they are trying to elicit a response from the other partner, it can be frustrating.

You can't force a partner to communicate with you. So, if you're getting the silent treatment in response to your efforts, the best advice is to give your partner some time to work through their emotions. Pushing for a response will only elicit a defensive backlash that serves no positive purpose.

Choosing the wrong time and place - If communication is something your partner struggles with, then the time and place for that conversation will make a big difference. Don't try to have a heart-to-heart if your partner isn't ready for it. Make sure both of you are emotionally open to the idea of communicating and choose a calm, safe environment that your partner knows well.

Not monitoring non-verbal cues - If your partner is giving you cues that they are starting to feel stressed or anxious during a conversation, take notice and ask them what they need. They may become overwhelmed by the fear they feel when opening up to someone else, so offer them that reassurance that you are there for them.

Chapter 6 – It All Starts with You

Taking the first steps toward healing your disorganized attachment style.

The time has come. You now have a clear understanding of what a disorganized attachment style is, how it develops, and why it is crippling your ability to feel safe in a relationship. What's left now is to find practical ways to heal your attachment style, move from insecure to secure in your interactions with other people, and better learn how to regulate the emotions that intimacy can trigger in you.

Emotions are a powerful thing, and for the person living with a disorganized attachment style, it can sometimes feel like your emotions rule your life and dictate your choices, even when you don't want them to. Individuals with a disorganized attachment respond to emotions in a different way than people with a secure attachment style. They might:

- Feel fear in moments of intimacy and closeness with another person, whether emotionally or physically

- Find it difficult to share their feelings with another person

- Might feel overwhelmed by emotions at times, and completely cut off from their emotions at other times

- May react unpredictably during moments of strong emotions

- Respond to emotional situations with anger

- May feel distrust of others who display emotions

- Might seek to close themselves off from people who reach out for a connection

- Truly want love, affection, and closeness from other people, but react with fear or anger when they receive it

This chapter is where you will learn the ways to begin to turn the corner. You can heal your disorganized attachment. You can move beyond your past trauma. And you can develop the kind of healthy, secure, rewarding relationships that you deserve.

You may struggle with self-soothing and self-regulation of your emotions – skills that should have developed in early childhood through positive, secure interactions with your caregivers. Without those vital skills, it can be easy to get caught in a whirlpool of emotions and feel like those emotions have power over your physical body, your choices and decisions, and your ability to build healthy relationships.

Disorganized attachment makes it hard to look at a situation objectively, weigh the pros and cons, work to understand other people's feelings and motivations, and clearly communicate with that other person. The powerful and extreme emotions you feel when put in certain situations simply get in the way. It's time to tame those emotions and start making better decisions for yourself.

Learning to Self-Regulate

Disorganized attachment can make someone feel out of control of both their situation and their reactions. We know that those reactions come as a result of a switched-on fear response that is left over from childhood trauma. That fear response results in powerful, overwhelming emotions. And that is something you may not be able to control, at least not right away. But what you can learn to do is find better ways to regulate those emotions, and therefore be able to make clearer decisions in the moment.

Self-regulation is a skill that we usually develop during early infancy and childhood. It works in much the same way that self-soothing does. We experience strong feelings of fear, uncertainty, and anxiety, and because of our positive experiences with parents or caregivers, we can regulate those emotions without fear. This ability develops because those caregivers respond to our needs in a positive way, by providing us with the things we need to be safe and secure. This builds a subconscious knowledge that even when those feelings arise because of an unmet need, we will not be stuck feeling them forever because help is on the way, just like it always is.

When our caregivers were unable or unwilling to respond to our needs in a positive way, instead offering anger, abuse, or neglect, then a negative association develops. We learn that when we ask for our needs to be met there's a chance that we will receive pain and fear in response, or sometimes no response at all. So, when those feelings develop in us as adults, we have no ability to self-soothe ourselves through them. Instead, we find ourselves crippled by fear and anxiety, with no way to help ourselves feel better.

Self-regulation involves finding ways to control the strong emotions that certain situations trigger within us as a result of prior trauma or abuse. When we can self-regulate, we are no longer a slave to those emotions and can make clear decisions and actions based on what's best for us rather than what our emotions dictate.

Being able to self-regulate is an important skill that adults need to be able to navigate the ups and downs of life. And it's vital for being able to maintain healthy relationships. When we can control our emotions and our reactions, we are better able to solve problems, communicate with people, and maintain a feeling of self-confidence and balance.

I also want to emphasize that learning to self-regulate your emotions is not the same as suppressing them. Those emotions are a part of you, and you can't simply wish them away. Suppressing your emotions is actually an unhealthy coping mechanism that can go hand in hand with disorganized attachment. There may be times when you shut down and close yourself off from others – and there may be times when those emotions explode and the people around you suffer the consequences.

Self-regulating means allowing yourself to feel those emotions, but at the same time gaining the ability to sit inside of them and really experience them – without those emotions dictating your actions or responses. It means finding ways to feel those emotions and still be okay. It means working to understand the reasons behind those emotions and the triggers that are driving your fear, anxiety, and anger. And then it means working to find practical ways to move forward and heal from some of those traumas that are tied to your emotional reactions.

People with a disorganized attachment style often find themselves unable to control their emotions, and unable to react appropriately to situations because of this. Instead of taking an action that benefits us and our partner in a healthy way, our emotions lead us to act rashly and take action that is only intended to do one thing - keep us safe.

Of course, everyone deserves to feel safe in their surroundings and in their interactions with other people. But the truth is that unless you are faced with a situation where you are suffering abuse at the hands of a partner, you are safe. You can remove yourself from situations that feel unhealthy or toxic. You have the ability to make decisions that will benefit you and your emotional well-being in the long run. Understanding that is the first step to being able to regulate your emotions.

Nobody is in complete control of their emotions - that's what makes emotions so powerful. If you are sad, you might find yourself crying even if you don't really want to. If you're scared, you might feel the urge to run away from whatever is causing that emotion. These are normal reactions to emotions, and stopping those feelings completely is not only impossible but unhealthy in the long run. Emotions are there for a reason.

The goal should be to find ways to manage those emotions. You can feel a certain way without letting those feelings dictate your responses and reactions.

So, how does an emotionally secure person react to strong emotions? They take practical steps to examine why they're feeling a certain way and how they can feel better. They try to find reasons for why those emotions might exist in the first place and then find ways to work through them without feeling stuck. They allow themselves to feel those emotions without letting them control their decisions.

Someone with a secure attachment style will be able to feel their emotions without succumbing to the urge to suppress them. They can feel strong emotions without experiencing angry, uncontrollable outbursts. They can express their feelings to others without feeling unsafe and fearful of the response they might get. And they can experience a whole range of emotions without allowing those feelings to dictate their choices.

Here's some practical advice on how to move through strong emotions constructively.

- Talk to someone you trust about how you are feeling.

- Use a journal to help you get those feelings out.

- Try meditation, visualization, or deep breathing exercises.

- Go for a walk, ride a bike, or get some exercise.

- Practice being mindful of your surroundings and situation in the present.

- Learn to step away without shutting down.

- Light some candles and take a relaxing bubble bath.

- Seek out a counselor or therapist.

Everyone will have a different way of dealing with strong emotions. The goal is to find a way to regulate those emotions yourself, instead of allowing those emotions to regulate you. People dealing with a disorganized attachment style might find it exceptionally hard to regulate their emotions because they sometimes feel anxious and sometimes feel avoidant. Because disorganized attachment is a mixture of anxious and avoidant attachment styles, they will flip-flop between states of emotion, making it harder to understand where those emotions are coming from and less able to figure out how to move past them.

Silencing Your Inner Voice

We all have an internal dialogue – that little voice in your head that seems to always have something to say. That inner voice is sometimes called our conscience, the inner part of ourselves that alerts us when something doesn't seem right. But it's more than that.

Our inner voice sometimes says things that make perfect sense and are useful for us. It can remind us when we're hungry or tired. It can remind us of things we need to accomplish during the day. It can help us remain focused on the things that are most important.

But our inner voice does more than just remind us of helpful things. In honesty, it often speaks directly to our subconscious insecurities. It echoes our feelings of inadequacy, feelings of low self-esteem, low self-worth, and all those inner fears that have deep-seated places in our being.

When our inner voice starts a monologue that is dictated by our fears, then it becomes less useful and even detrimental to our emotional health. And if we learn to listen to it during those times, then we are likely to lose control of our emotions and make decisions based on those emotions.

To silence that inner voice, you need to find ways to correct it when you recognize that the information it is giving you is biased and incorrect. That inner dialogue is often directly connected to our fear response, and subconsciously we might believe that the inner voice has our best interests at heart. But thinking in this way is a mistake and will only wind up with us being stuck inside that fear response when we no longer need to be.

Let's go through some of those critical, fear-based thoughts your inner voice might be telling you.

"Everyone is going to hurt me eventually."

"If I open up to someone, they will be able to use my feelings against me."

"My partner is going to cheat on me because I'm not good enough."

"It would be safer if I were just alone."

"Nobody will ever be able to love me the way I am."

"I'm just not good enough."

"I fail at everything, and I will fail at this relationship too."

"There must be something wrong with me that I can't make a relationship work."

These thoughts are all fear-based and only result in you feeling bad about yourself. In order to move past these thoughts, you must practice putting that inner voice in its proper place by recognizing when the things it is telling you are completely wrong.

Let's look at how we can respond to these inner thoughts in a constructive way.

Inner voice: *"Everyone is going to hurt me eventually."*

Correction: *"There are lots of people in my life who have never hurt me, and there are lots of good people in the world who won't hurt me."*

Inner thought: *"If I open up to someone, they will be able to use my feelings against me."*

Correction: *"Opening up emotionally to someone puts me in no actual danger."*

Inner voice: *"My partner is going to cheat on me because I'm just not good enough."*

Correction: *"My partner has never given me any reason to suspect them of cheating, and I am good enough for someone to love me unconditionally."*

Inner voice: *"It would be safer if I were just alone."*

Correction: *"Being in a healthy relationship poses no threat to my well-being and being alone is not what I want for myself."*

Inner voice: *"Nobody will ever be able to love me the way I am."*

Correction: *"I am a good person with many amazing qualities, and I deserve to be loved."*

Inner voice: *"I'm just not good enough."*

Correction: *"I am good enough just the way I am. Nobody is perfect."*

Inner voice: *"I fail at everything, and I will fail at this relationship too."*

Correction: *"I have had many successes in my life, and I can have a successful relationship as well."*

Inner voice: *"There must be something wrong with me that I can't make a relationship work."*

Correction: *"Relationships are hard work, but I can learn to create a trusting connection with another person."*

Learning that your inner voice is often coming from a place of internalized fear and the expectation of pain can help you understand that that voice is wrong. It's not telling you the whole truth and there may be hidden emotions of fear and the expectation that closeness and intimacy will automatically lead to pain. Use this knowledge to begin correcting that pesky inner voice when it starts creeping into your thoughts. Doing so will help you reprogram that internal dialogue to one that promotes inner peace and self-confidence. Start telling yourself that you are enough, you are worth it, and you are safe. Eventually, you will start to believe it.

Is It Time for Therapy?

Asking for help when you need it most is something that individuals living with a disorganized attachment style might struggle with. That's because putting yourself out there as vulnerable is scary and sometimes feels like you're placing yourself in a dangerous situation.

However, seeking professional counseling or therapy for your disorganized attachment can be extremely beneficial for some people. This is especially true if you suffered through physical, emotional, verbal, or sexual abuse. Traumatic experiences like those can leave long-lasting, deep-seated scars that you might not even realize are there.

Therapy provides a neutral ground that can feel like a safe space for people with disorganized attachment, or at least safer than opening up to someone in our own lives. That's because you walk into therapy with the knowledge that the therapist is a trained, medical professional whose job it is to listen to your problems without judgment. They are a neutral party and the therapist's office is neutral ground. Even if you open up completely behind those closed doors, you might feel safer knowing you can prop those barrier walls back up when you leave.

Therapy can allow you the time and space to explore your emotions, fears, and trauma responses in a safe and judgment-free zone. And therapists can help equip you with the tools and knowledge you need to move forward in a healthy way.

Moving past the fear and emotions tied to our past trauma often requires facing that trauma head-on. This can be an incredibly scary and stressful experience for many people. That's why having the assistance of a professional to help you navigate those emotions, find practical ways to cope and check up on your progress can be helpful.

Therapists also provide a sounding board for your thoughts. If you are struggling with your own actions and reactions, you can share them with your therapist and expect an honest answer. And because therapists are a third party, they are able to gain a greater perspective on your overall situation. They can help explain why you're feeling certain emotions, and why you react in a certain way.

Start Building Healthy Relationships

Building healthy relationships starts with you – and that means putting yourself out there. People with disorganized attachments often have difficulty forming relationships of all kinds. They might have a rocky history with close family members because of a fall-out from the past. They might have fractured friendships or strained connections with people in their lives.

The best way to learn how to build a healthy relationship is simply to build one! Take steps to repair those broken family relationships, find time to reconnect with friends, and make an effort to make new connections. Focus on creating open, trusting bonds with secure, well-adjusted people who will be able to support you in your efforts and return your love in a positive way.

Once you start building those positive bonds with the people closest to you and learn how to forge new bonds outside of your safe circle, you will start to realize how great a trusting, reciprocal relationship can be. You will start to create new associations between openness and connections to peace, happiness, and joy, instead of associating those things with pain and fear. Little by little, you will start to heal.

Sharing Your Disorganized Attachment Style with Others

Now that you understand that your reactions and emotions are often a direct result of abuse, neglect, and trauma suffered during early childhood, it will be easier to understand when those truths affect the way you interact with people as an adult. But that doesn't mean the other people in your life will automatically understand these things. And most people don't want to walk through the remainder of their lives wearing a sign around their neck that reads, "I have a disorganized attachment, ask me how!"

Sharing your experiences and feelings with other people is a very personal decision, and every person will approach the task in a different way. And that is perfectly okay. What works for one person might not work for someone else.

Because disorganized attachment causes you to feel vulnerable and fearful of sharing your emotions and feelings with someone else, it can be even harder to share the fact that you have an insecure attachment. But here's the good news. As you start to heal and find better ways to regulate your emotions, it will get easier.

Not every person you encounter in your life needs to hear a disclaimer from you. But in certain situations, you might feel like opening up about your attachment issues will benefit both you and the other people in your life. And you might be surprised at how willing other people are to listen and how understanding of your feelings they are.

Remember, everyone has issues, and while the disorganized attachment style is considered the rarest of the three, attachment styles themselves are not all that rare. As a matter of fact, they are fairly common.

When it comes to sharing information about past trauma and abuse, that can be more difficult for most people, and that makes sense. But in honesty, deciding to share that very personal information is not entirely necessary in helping someone understand what a disorganized attachment really is. What's more important is helping them understand how your insecure attachment style can affect the way you react to intimacy, uncertainty, or situations that make you feel fearful. That's part of the issue they will likely see and experience, and that's the part that matters right now.

Doing the Deep Work

There's a lot of actual science behind how an insecure attachment style develops. Our internalized reactions aren't intangible things that only exist in theory. They are rooted in our very brains - wired into our neurological systems and autonomic nervous systems.

Changing the pattern of behavior and emotions that are deeply seated in our physical bodies is challenging, more so than you might realize. It will take a dedicated effort, repeated reinforcement, and lots of practice to rewire your brain and reset your internal fear response. But it can be done, and there is hope that you can heal.

The human body exists as a combination of mind, body, and spirit. These three manifestations of our being come together to form our whole selves. In order to heal and move past a disorganized attachment style, you must heal each part of yourself individually and then slowly reintegrate the parts of yourself into a new and healthier structure. That's because each of these parts of yourself is interconnected and each part is reliant on every other part.

Your mind houses a lot of the learned beliefs that stem from those traumatic experiences you lived through as a child. Your brain developed to expect pain and fear in response to certain situations, and those associations are deeply embedded into your subconscious reactions. Learning to sever those negative associations learned as infants and build new and positive associations is a huge part of healing an insecure attachment style.

Your mind directs your body to feel a certain way in response to stress and fear. A racing pulse, a pounding heart, sweaty palms, trembling – these are all common physical manifestations of stress and anxiety and often accompany strong emotions stirred up by triggers. Learning to work through the physical symptoms that follow triggers and emotions can help you feel more in control of your body and better able to regulate your response to those emotions.

Your spirit is the unseen part of your inner self – that part that holds your hopes and dreams for the future - your ambition, your passion, and your drive to succeed. Reprogramming your spirit to expect good things will create scenarios where you unconsciously pull those good things toward yourself instead of constantly circling negative thoughts and emotions.

Therapy or counseling is a great tool that is always an option if you find yourself struggling with this part of your healing process. Professional therapists will be able to walk you through the process and give you tools to heal those past wrongs in a healthy way so that you can move forward.

Chapter 7 – You Become What You Think

Finding ways to improve your perception of yourself, improve your self-worth, and be more confident.

Going through your adult life while dragging a disorganized attachment along with you is no way to live. A lot of the emotions and fear surrounding the person with a disorganized attachment style are the result of internalized trauma. You feel like you are the drama and the result of you not being worthy of honest, open, safe, and accepting love from other people is your fault.

But you shouldn't have to feel that way, and in reality, these feelings aren't true. They are a result of the abuse, neglect, and trauma that you suffered as a child.

Trauma and abuse victims often develop feelings of low self-esteem and a damaged sense of self-worth. This can result from repeated exposure to abusive environments, and the inability of the young infant or child to rationalize the reasons for that abuse. Without any way to understand a caregiver's motivations or the factors that result in a caregiver being abusive or neglectful, a young human being is left with no choice but to put the blame on themselves. They internalize anger and negative emotions, believing themselves to be unworthy of any other kind of attention.

These can be powerful feelings that are difficult to overcome, especially when coupled with the see-saw of emotions that a disorganized attachment often brings. But recognizing the underlying factors behind your low self-worth is the first step to correcting it.

What is Self-Worth, Really?

Self-worth is one of those phrases that people tend to throw around without really understanding what it means. It is actually interchangeable with the terms "self-esteem" and "self-image." All of these terms are used to describe a sense of our own value as human beings. They are measurements we use to describe our value as compared to others in the world - a description of how we perceive ourselves. We develop our self-worth over years and years, starting during our earliest childhood experiences.

An individual with high self-esteem or high self-worth has a belief that they are valuable as human beings, and therefore are deserving of good things. And a person with low self-esteem or self-worth believes themselves to be unworthy of good things. They feel as if they are deserving of negative things and negative outcomes in their lives because they hold a belief that their personal value is beneath that of others.

Developing a low sense of personal value can inhibit your life, leading you to steer clear of choices and decisions that might seem too difficult but would otherwise improve your life, such as taking a new job or making new friends. Having a low sense of worth can affect the choices you make on a daily basis, how you dress, how you take care of your body, your food choices, and your personal hygiene.

People with low self-worth might not think themselves valuable enough to be worth the effort. They might forgo exercise and healthy eating habits, or they might develop eating disorders. They might not bother to care for their personal appearance, because deep down they feel as if they will never be good enough anyhow, no matter how much effort they put in.

When you have low self-worth, you might develop an inferiority complex. This condition is common among individuals who grew up with parents who exhibited overbearing expectations but also results from a history of trauma or abuse.

How to Boost Your Self-Worth

Holding preconceived notions about your self-worth is damaging to your overall well-being. Those feelings of inadequacy and low self-esteem are hard to shake, but it is not impossible. Here are some ways you can start to reprogram your sense of self-worth.

1. Make a list of all your positive qualities and accomplishments. It can be all too easy to focus on what you feel are your shortcomings, and not give enough attention to the good parts of you. Get as detailed as you can with your list. Include any physical characteristics you like about yourself, skills and talents you feel you possess, unique qualities that make you who you are, and any accomplishments or experiences you have had. Remember those compliments that you receive from other people as well, because others often see us more clearly than we see ourselves.

2. Take a long look at yourself in the mirror every morning, or whenever you start feeling down on yourself. Recognize all of those qualities and characteristics from your list that you like about yourself. Take a picture of yourself when you find a moment when you look and feel good and be sure to include a great big smile! Hang that picture

somewhere you can see it every day and use it as a reminder that you are valuable.

3. Ask your close friends and family what they think your best qualities are. You might be surprised at what they have to say! If you're comfortable sharing your feelings with someone else, simply explain that you are working on building up your self-esteem and this is an exercise that can help you on your journey.

4. Don't compare yourself with others. Every single person on this planet is unique and different. We have different skills, different talents, and different experiences. And it's the combination of these things that makes us who we are. Comparing yourself to someone else serves no purpose, especially because you are only seeing what's on the surface of that other person. You have no knowledge of how they view themselves, their internal motivations, or their feelings. So although other people may appear to have it all together, chances are they have their own shortcomings and struggles. Everyone is different and everyone has value, even you!

5. Recognize that you have value, and your needs are important. Actively work to do things for yourself that will make you feel a little bit better, even if they are small things. Don't be afraid to put yourself and your needs first, say no when something doesn't

feel right, and take actions that will improve your self-image.

Building Your Confidence

Confidence and self-worth go hand in hand. When you see yourself as having value and being capable of success, you will be more likely to feel secure and safe enough to put yourself out there and take risks. And this doesn't mean bungee jumping or cliff diving kind of risks, but instead the kind we face every day in our lives.

When you have confidence, you can put yourself in situations and scenarios where you have a potential risk of hurt or disappointment. And you can do so without worrying about the outcome because you know that failure, although always a possibility, is not the end of the world. Every failure and shortfall serves a purpose. It builds our knowledge, improves our skills, and hardens our resolve so that the next time we try, and try again, we get a little better every time.

Confidence needs to come from inside yourself. It's something you have always had the capacity for, even if it doesn't feel that way now. Think back to your school days. How many times did you fail at something before finally succeeding? The answer is likely quite a few. That's because life is a learning experience, and nobody gets it right the first time, every time. Life is a series of experiences and every single one has value. Below are a few examples of exercises that can help you improve your confidence.

1. Don't underestimate yourself. It can sometimes be tempting to avoid things we deem difficult because we feel as if we are simply not good enough to succeed. But if you look back on your past experiences, you will discover there were many instances where you did succeed. And even moments when you "knocked it out of the park!" Try to judge each situation on its own merits and appreciate the fact that you are capable of great things.

2. Think positively. I know, this seems like such a simple thing and it's easier said than done. Our inner voice tends to be our biggest critic, and it can creep in whispering doubts and reminders of our past failures at the most critical moments. Don't listen to it. Positive thinking means silencing that inner critic and replacing it with a cheerleader. Be your own biggest fan and remind yourself that you can do hard things. Be the "little engine that could," and phrase your inner thoughts with "I can," instead of "I can't."

3. Set yourself up for success. This one is more of a preparation for success because having confidence is a feeling that will be easier to internalize if you can see the proof in your abilities

for yourself. Saying you will succeed and positioning yourself in the best possible scenario to for success are two different things. You have to put in the work first. Study extra hard. Show up early. Put in that extra effort. Doing some prep work will ensure you have a better chance of getting what it is you want, and after a few times of seeing that equation in action, you will start to believe it, and live it.

4. Set small goals and work to achieve them. If making big jumps is too overwhelming for you, set smaller goals first. Once you see how capable you are of achieving those goals, no matter how small the size, your confidence will start to grow. Try to reach one small goal every day. Create a vision board or use a journal to really visualize your goals. Include the small ones you will work to achieve every day, and also the big ones you would like to reach in the future. Mark your success so you can see your results in action!

5. Change your physical habits to exact a change in how you feel inside. Even the action of taking a shower every morning, going for that run before breakfast, or fixing your hair or makeup. These simple strategies can make a huge difference to how you feel during the day. Try to stand up tall, smile when meeting new people, and use direct eye contact. Speak clearly and concisely. All of

these things will serve to improve your self-image and your confidence will get a boost as a result!

Overcoming Your Fears

Fear can be debilitating, especially when it's an internalized response left over from childhood abuse and trauma. In a general sense, fear serves an actual purpose. It's an emotion designed to alert us to danger. But when it arises in response to situations that actually pose no threat, then it is no longer useful and instead becomes an emotion that holds us back.

Allowing fear to stop you from progressing in your life or going after those things you truly want, such as healthy relationships, can damage your self-esteem and confidence even more. It sets you up for failure, because you will back away from opening up to people, push people away from you, or try to avoid confrontation. As the saying goes, "You miss 100% of the shots you don't take."

Let's review some of the ways to overcome your fears. Doing so will allow you to start reaching for those things you really want and need.

1. Find an emotional outlet. Fear can manifest itself through physical symptoms. When you start feeling those symptoms, it is a sign that your fear is

trying to get the best of you. Finding an emotional outlet or some activity that distracts your mind can help reset your mind before it gets trapped in the fear cycle.

2. Deep breathing is a great tool that can help calm you in moments where fear leads to panic. Even a few deep breaths can make a world of difference when feelings of fear, panic, and anxiety start to set in.

3. Imagine the worst thing that could possibly happen - the thing you are most afraid of at the moment. Then compare that thought with what is actually happening. In doing so, you will realize that your worst fear is unfounded. There's no point in being afraid of something that is not actually happening right now.

4. Use visualization and meditation to calm yourself through moments of extreme fear. Mentally put yourself in a happy place and your body's responses to the fear you are feeling will slowly dissipate.

5. Talk about your fears with someone close to you. This can be easier said than done for people who have a disorganized attachment because opening up is one of the things that causes a fear response in the first place. But even sharing a little bit about how you are feeling with someone you really trust

will allow you to unburden yourself. Those inner thoughts that are driving your fear will lose some of their power when you vocalize them to another person. If you don't have someone you trust enough to open up to, try to speak your fears out loud to yourself or write them down.

Learning to Trust Again

People with disorganized attachment have a damaged ability to trust those around them. Past experiences have taught them that people are not to be trusted and doing so puts them in a place of vulnerability where they are likely to be hurt.

A healthy, secure relationship requires a sense of trust on the part of both people. You can't know what your partner is thinking 100% of the time, no matter how much you might want to. You can't know if they truly love you like they say they do. You can't know if they are thinking of leaving the relationship or cheating with another person. You can't know if they are lying or telling the truth.

In a relationship built on trust, you will be able to love your partner and open yourself up to them without actually knowing all of those things because you will trust that other person. You will be able to be your authentic self around your partner, feel safe and secure with that person, and believe that they have your best interests at heart. That's what trust is.

Trust is a difficult thing to rebuild once it has been broken. Feeling betrayed or hurt by another person to whom you opened yourself up is a terrible thing, and the feelings created by a broken trust may linger even after you have forgiven that betrayal. That's how it feels to have a disorganized attachment style, except that the feeling of broken trust is present and we assign those feelings to people even when they don't deserve it. But there are ways you can overcome those feelings.

1. Don't rush yourself. Building trust takes time. Building an open, healthy relationship will require you to truly trust that the other person won't hurt you. But it doesn't need to happen all at once. If you need to pace yourself and open up a little bit at a time, then do so.

2. Communicate with your partner! Communication is a key factor in relationships, and without effective communication, you will have a hard time allowing yourself to trust. And speaking openly about how you are feeling will help your partner better understand where you're coming from, especially in moments where you feel the need to hold back or pull away.

3. Don't confuse trust with control. People with disorganized attachment often act out or exhibit

extreme emotions as a way to maintain control of situations where they feel vulnerable. These feelings can often result from feelings of mistrust. Understand that trusting your partner is not the same thing as having complete control over your partner's actions or responses. When you can relinquish some control and come to a neutral ground with your partner, then you can start to build trust.

4. Be trustworthy yourself! If you expect to build trust in a relationship, it will be important that you act in trustworthy ways yourself. Otherwise, you are sabotaging your efforts. Being trustworthy means more than just being honest and not telling lies. It means being forthcoming about how you are feeling.

5. Learn to trust yourself! In an effort to build your confidence and self-worth, you will need to learn to trust your own reactions. This doesn't mean succumbing to the feelings of fear that arise as a result of your disorganized attachment. In fact, it means really stripping away those preconceptions and identifying the underlying reasons for your behavior. Trust that you are able to move past your trauma and build a better future for yourself.

Building Trust with Someone Else

Building trust is a slow process that takes time and practice, especially when it feels foreign and unfamiliar to you. That inner voice might be constantly telling you that people aren't to be trusted, that they will all hurt you eventually, and that you're better off shutting them out. It's not true. That's not to guarantee that every single person in the world has your best interests at heart and will be completely honest with you 100% of the time. Unfortunately, the world simply doesn't work that way.

What you need to realize is that having someone betray you or break your trust is a terrible feeling, but it doesn't present a risk of actual harm. People with a disorganized attachment style associate feelings of mistrust with abuse and trauma because their first experiences trusting another person had terrible outcomes. But that won't be true the majority of the time, and you are no longer at the mercy of someone else's actions. You are a fully-grown, capable adult with the ability to walk away from potentially threatening situations.

Here are some tips on **how to slowly build trust with another person.**

1. Don't be the hall monitor in the relationship. People with trust issues sometimes over-monitor their partner's actions, keeping tabs on where they are and what they're doing at all times of the day. This behavior can help people feel more at ease because they feel like they will be better able to detect when a partner is lying, or if they suspect a

partner of dishonesty already and are fishing for proof. Give your partner the benefit of the doubt unless or until they give you a reason to think otherwise.

2. Don't throw around accusations. If you have a solid reason to doubt your partner's motives or actions, speak to them openly about it. Remember to approach them in a non-confrontational manner, explaining why you feel the way you do. Lobbing unfounded accusations at them is likely to build a wall between you that will make it harder to communicate openly and lead to even more mistrust. Your partner might feel like they might as well do exactly what you're accusing them of since you think they have already done so anyhow.

3. Be your own person. Remember that being a partner in a relationship is not all that you are. If every thought and action surrounds trying to build that relationship, it can lead to hyperfocus that may feel overwhelming for your partner. Don't lose yourself in the pursuit of that relationship.

4. Confront the reasons leading you to not trust your partner. Examine the reasons you might feel the way you do. If your partner is exhibiting a certain behavior that triggers feelings of mistrust in you, ask yourself why. Are they actually doing or saying something that deserves your mistrust? Or is it simply your fear telling you that they deserve your

mistrust? Speaking openly to your partner about the reasons behind your feelings will help you both better understand where the other person is coming from.

5. Consider couples therapy. Therapy is a great way for two people to speak openly about their feelings and deal with any emotions that might arise in the process. Healing trauma can be a messy process, and without the right tools and guidance to get through it can lead to strong emotions that confuse and cloud the situation. A counselor or therapist can help you and your partner work through issues together and provide practical advice that will help you improve your communication and your relationship.

Healing is a Journey – Start with a Single Step

Abuse, neglect, and trauma can have long-lasting effects on people, creating complicated, tangled emotions that develop over time. It will take just as long to untangle those emotions and find a better way forward. It can be done, but it will require you to put in the real work. And that starts with taking the first step.

The good news is that you are in complete control of your future. You make your own choices and control your own reactions, even when it might feel like you are at the mercy of your emotions. Follow the advice listed about building a better you, starting by improving your self-image, recognizing your self-worth, and building your confidence. Only then will you be able to realize that you are able to improve your life by making better choices and actively working to build better relationships. In the next chapter, we will paint a picture of just what that healthy, open relationship might look like.

Chapter 8 – Secure Attachment Should Feel This Way

What a secure, healthy relationship can look and feel like, and why having one can be one of the best parts of living.

You likely picked up this book in hopes of either healing your own attachment issues or as a way to better understand your partner's disorganized attachment style. I hope that in reading through the contents of this book you now have a clearer understanding of exactly what disorganized attachment is, how it develops in people, and how it can negatively affect our interpersonal relationships.

The goal of working through the fears and anxieties that come with a disorganized attachment is to be able to build healthier relationships, whether it is with close friends, family members, or romantic partners. There are lots of people who go about their adult lives with no attachment issues or, put another way, with the ability to build secure attachments with people.

What exactly is a secure attachment and what does it look like in the context of a relationship? And why should we want to have that kind of attachment to begin with? Let's take a closer look at what a secure attachment comes from and why a healthy relationship built between people with a secure attachment style is ideal for many people.

Feeling Secure Starts Early

Security, or the state of being secure, when referring to objects means to be fixed or fastened so as not to give way, become loose, or be lost. In other terms, such as how we apply it to our attachment style, it means not being subject to threat, or certain to remain and continue safe and unharmed. It means feeling safe, stable, and free from fear and anxiety.

When we look at the definition of the word secure, it can be easy to see how having those feelings described above would benefit someone in their adult life. And how feeling secure can make it easier to form lasting bonds with other people.

Feeling insecure means you feel at risk because of the threat of things or people around you. You feel like the people you encounter pose a threat and are capable of hurting you either emotionally or physically. And in reality, that is very true. You cannot control other people's actions, emotions, or reactions. But as adults, we have the ability to recognize when we are actually at risk and take direct action to remedy our situation.

The Secure Infant/Caregiver Dynamic

Nobody's relationship with their parents or caregivers is ever perfect. That's because no child is perfect, and no adult is perfect either. There will be bumpy roads and bad days along the way. Caregivers will make mistakes and do things they wish they could take back.

Overall, a caregiver who is present, both emotionally and physically, will be able to raise a child who is able to develop a secure attachment with other people. A secure attachment style develops when a child has a healthy, responsive relationship with at least one caregiver. That child will learn through positive experiences that they can ask for help and receive it without any negative reaction. They learn it is safe to communicate their needs. They learn that feelings of distress, fear, pain, and anxiety are only temporary and will resolve eventually because a caregiver will meet their needs. This allows them to learn important life skills like self-soothing and how to regulate their emotions.

You have likely encountered infants and children at some point in their life and have seen a secure attachment at work. A child with a secure attachment might show distress or uncertainty when separated from a caregiver but will calm down when that caregiver returns. Sort of like when parents leave a child in the care of a babysitter for an evening. The child might cry when the parents leave, at least the first few times, and then be happy and overjoyed when the parents return at the end of the night.

A secure child who is experiencing fear or distress will be able to accept love and comfort from their caregiver and feel calmer and more secure as a result of that love. A secure child will be comfortable exploring their world, taking risks with their environment in an effort to learn about the people and things around them, because they have an inherent knowledge that their caregiver will be around to keep them safe and pick them up if they stumble. They know these things because they have seen them happen before. They have seen true love and support in action.

These qualities developed from knowing you have a reliable caregiver who is present and able to offer consistent support to follow you into adulthood. These are the experiences that shape the way you to view the world around you, and set your expectations of how other people will treat you and the way you approach relationships. They literally shape the person you become, and having a sense of security in early childhood allows you to feel that same sense of security as an adult.

People with a secure attachment style have a better sense of self, are able to form close relationships with others, and are able to accept love and affection from people in their lives. Below are some traits that are commonly found in adults with a secure attachment style.

- Ability to self-regulate emotions

- Good coping skills

- Can communicate and express both physical and emotional needs

- Comfortable with physical and emotional intimacy

- Approach difficulties in relationships in a proactive manner

- Clearly set and hold to personal boundaries with others

- Comfortable both giving and receiving love from others

- Have greater self-confidence and an improved self-image

What Secure Attachment Looks Like

A relationship between two people with a secure attachment style looks much different from what you are probably used to. But once you have experienced the love, empathy, and support that is provided by such a relationship you will understand exactly why people strive so hard to find a bond like this.

A healthy relationship involves two people who feel 100% safe and secure with each other, even when they are completely exposed and vulnerable. Two securely attached partners will be able to offer each other comfort and support in those times when it's needed the most. And they will do so without feeling the need to criticize their partner, blame them for their mistakes, or shame them for their feelings.

A healthy relationship features two partners who are able to communicate openly with each other. They can share their innermost thoughts and feelings without fear of rejection or ridicule. They can work together through problems and difficulties that arise in the relationship or in each other's lives. They can do these things transparently and calmly because they know wholeheartedly that the other person has their best interests in mind and won't do or say anything intended to cause pain.

A healthy relationship involves two individuals, with their own desires and interests, who just happen to come together to love and support one another. They are able to safely and securely explore their own interests and be their own person without causing their partner to feel uncertainty or jealousy. And they can build a life or relationship together without having to sacrifice any part of themselves. A secure relationship adds something to your life instead of subtracting anything from who you already are or who you want to be in the future.

A healthy relationship includes two partners who can ask for help when they need it and know, without a doubt, that their partner will be there to support them. There is no fear of rejection and no worry that they will be left out in the cold because a secure partner is always there when they're needed the most.

A healthy relationship involves trust and respect. Both partners can trust each other 100% of the time without any underlying fear that the other person is secretly plotting against them or will hurt them eventually. These relationships are based on the reality of what actually happens in the context of the relationship rather than unfounded fears about what might happen.

A healthy relationship happens between two secure individuals who love each other and want only the best for each other, both in the relationship itself and on a personal level. They will support each other's ambitions and dreams, help them navigate their fears and uncertainties, and work together to build the kind of future both partners desire.

Look for Healthy Relationships

Another way to start healing is by purging your life of relationships that are toxic or counterproductive to your journey. People with disorganized attachment are often drawn to those people who have their own insecure attachment style. It's the "like attracts like" theory. Unfortunately, that situation is not conducive to helping you work on your own issues at all. Instead, it's more likely you will find yourself stuck in a seemingly never-ending cycle of anxiety, fear, jealousy, and anger.

When you have disorganized attachment and are in a relationship with someone who has their own insecure attachment issue, that person will likely be unable to give you what you need to heal – which is openness, honest communication, empathy, compassion, support, and stability. Instead, they will only offer more of the same thing you are already dealing with, which gets you nowhere and gets your partner nowhere as well.

And maybe you're thinking to yourself, "Well, if I can fix my attachment issues then I can fix my partner's attachment problems too!" I beg you not to take on a project like that if you are still working to fix your own attachment issues. You need to focus on healing your own attachment problems first – only then will you have the clarity of mind and emotion to tackle helping someone else with their problems.

It's important to remember that toxic relationships aren't just between two romantic partners. There could be relationships with friends and acquaintances, family members, coworkers, and other people you encounter regularly in your life. And in some instances, you might not be able to completely sever those relationships, especially when family bonds keep you tied to someone.

But that doesn't mean you can't redefine those relationships, set boundaries for yourself, and clearly communicate those boundaries with the other person. This action needs to come from a desire for healing for yourself, and not from the typical knee-jerk reaction that people with disorganized attachment often feel. By this point, you should be able to understand how that fear-based reaction works and clearly understand which relationships are hindering your growth more than helping you along your journey.

Building a Secure Relationship

If a happy, healthy, secure relationship sounds like exactly what you need in your life, then it's time to start looking for one. Understand that you will need to do a lot of hard work on yourself in order to be a secure partner in the relationship, and you will need to look for a partner who is secure. This is the ideal formula for a healthy relationship. Look to build a relationship with someone who exhibits the following characteristics:

- A partner who respects your personal space and privacy

- A partner who respects your right to build relationships with friends and family without them needing to be included every time

- A partner who makes you feel safe and comfortable during communication

- A partner who never makes you feel physically or emotionally unsafe

- A partner who doesn't try to control your actions or decisions

- A partner who is willing to negotiate, compromise, and work through issues as a team

- A partner who goes out of their way to make you feel special or show you affection

- A partner who is honest and secure enough in themselves to never doubt your actions or motivations

Building a secure relationship isn't something that will happen overnight. It takes time and practice on both sides. And both partners will probably make mistakes along the way. After all, nobody is perfect and the same holds true for people involved in any kind of relationship.

The key is to build the kind of relationship where those mistakes don't automatically lead to an implosion. Two securely attached partners can come together to work through problems when they arise without feeling threatened or fearful in the process. When you have built a relationship based on mutual respect, trust, compassion, and care for the other person, then you have a healthy, secure relationship.

A secure relationship and the right partner are out there – somewhere – for everyone. But before you can build this kind of relationship with someone else you will need to face your own disorganized attachment issues. If you already have a relationship with someone who is secure and stable in their attachment style, then you are in a good position to heal, and you get the benefit of your partner's unwavering support.

If you're currently single and are looking for a secure relationship, it's important to work on yourself first. Start small and give yourself the time and space to heal correctly. Don't rush into things without having stable ground under your feet first. You can't love someone else until you love yourself first.

Conclusion – Time to Move Forward

If you are living with a disorganized attachment style and are hoping to improve your interpersonal relationship skills so you can build better, healthier relationships, then reading this book is a great first step. Educating yourself about disorganized attachment and what it means for you going forward will help you untangle the emotions that come along with it. And in this book, we have discussed the practical steps you can take to help you start to heal your trauma and get to where you want to be in life.

Self-Healing

The first step is learning how to actively work on yourself. By learning about your insecure attachment style and how your past trauma and experiences are coloring your emotions and decisions now. Once you are armed with that knowledge, it will be easier to recognize when your actions and reactions to a partner or situation are coming from a place of fear because of your disorganized attachment. That way you can take a step back from the situation, take a few deep breaths, and make a better decision based on the actual circumstances and not just your learned fear-based reaction to the things around you.

Build a Better You

Building your self-esteem and growing your sense of self-worth is one of the most important steps on your healing journey. Your self-worth has probably been heavily damaged by your past childhood experiences, even if you don't realize the extent of the damage. You likely grew up feeling partially responsible for the abuse or neglect you suffered as an infant or child. You internalize feelings of inadequacy because you had no other way to justify the things that were done to you at such a young age.

Undoing those negative thoughts and firmly held beliefs about yourself will take a lot of hard work and lots of time. It will require you to take steps every day designed to reprogram your mind and teach it that you do have great worth, you are a good person with lots of fabulous qualities, and you do deserve good things in your life. Once you start to do that it will be easier to gain enough confidence in yourself to really go after the things you want, without letting your fear of failure creep in and ruin it for you.

Find a Support System

It's important that you don't try to face every single problem on your own, and that includes healing from your disorganized attachment - because you have likely lived most of your life up to this point trying to do exactly that. Disorganized attachment can cause people to develop an incorrect association between communicating a need and pain or fear. And it's that incorrect association that prevents us from opening up to people in our lives who truly care about us and want to help us feel better.

Try to identify at least one or two people in your life who you fully trust. Reach out to those people for support and understanding. If you're not completely comfortable baring your whole soul with someone right away, that's entirely okay. Nobody expects a complete turnaround of behaviors that have been built up over decades of living. Instead look to build a healthy relationship with that person slowly, one step at a time if necessary. Spend time together just hanging out or doing activities that you both find fun and relaxing. Be in close proximity to someone who doesn't pose a threat to you physically or emotionally. Eventually, you will start to feel more comfortable with the idea of opening up and sharing your feelings and emotions.

Heal your Inner-Child

A large part of healing from a disorganized attachment style is tied to healing from the abuse, neglect, and trauma that triggered the issue in the first place. You can't heal the consequences without dealing with the source – and for you, that source is likely filled with unhappy and painful recollections.

Healing from trauma is no easy feat. The other things mentioned in this list and the tips found in this book are some good first steps along the way. But don't expect to wake up one day and suddenly feel like you are healed. It simply doesn't work that way for most people.

Trauma and abuse can hold a powerful grip on people and certain triggers can lead you right back to the feelings and emotions of those experiences. Healing from that trauma means understanding that you were not to blame for the abuse, neglect, or trauma you were subjected to as an infant or child. The caregivers around you failed at their job of providing you with a safe, secure environment designed to give you the tools and space to develop as a well-rounded and well-adjusted adult.

Time to Move Forward

Now that you have all the tools and knowledge you need to heal your past trauma and build better relationships – go out there and use them! Remember that your attachment style is not a permanent fixture in your life and can be changed with time and practice. Achieving a secure attachment style requires patience and consistency – but it can be done, and you deserve it.

I hope that by reading this book you can now feel safe and secure taking those first few steps toward a better future for yourself. If you enjoyed this book and found it useful, please leave a review on Amazon! And remember that only you can change your future.

Don't just finish reading this book and then set it aside. Actually, take some of the tips you read here and implement them in your own life. You will be amazed at the difference in the way you feel about yourself. I hope that this book has sparked a desire inside of you to really go after all the great things you deserve for yourself. Thank you so much for reading, and here's to you and your future!

References

(2022.). *Disorganized Attachment Style Can Explain Why Some People Run Hot*. Women's Health Magazine. https://www.womenshealthmag.com/relationships/a400 79652/disorganized-attachment-style/

(n.d.). *How Attachment Styles Affect Adult Relationships*. HelpGuide.org. https://www.helpguide.org/articles/relationships-communication/attachment-and-adult-relationships.htm

(2021). *What is Disorganized Attachment in Relationships*. Marriage.com. https://www.marriage.com/advice/mental-health/disorganized-attachment-in-relationships/

(2021). *Disorganized Attachment in Relationships*. The Attachment Project. https://www.attachmentproject.com/disorganized-attachment-relationships/

(2019). *Helping Someone With a Disorganized Attachment Style*. sounds true. https://resources.soundstrue.com/blog/helping-someone-with-a-disorganized-attachment-style/

(2020). *Ten Ways to Fight Your Fears.* NHS Inform. https://www.nhsinform.scot/healthy-living/mental-wellbeing/fears-and-phobias/ten-ways-to-fight-your-fears

(2021). *How to Work Through Your Relationship Fears.* PsychCentral. https://psychcentral.com/health/dont-let-fear-destroy-your-relationship

(2009). *7 Ways to Heal Your Childhood Trauma.* CASAPALMERA. https://casapalmera.com/blog/7-ways-to-heal-your-childhood-trauma/

(2019). *9 Ways to Feel More Present With Your Partner, According to Experts.* Bustle. https://www.bustle.com/p/9-ways-to-feel-more-present-with-your-partner-according-to-experts-15954342

(2021). *A Deep Dive Into Disorganized Attachment.* Thrive Family Services. https://thrivefamilyservices.com/a-deep-dive-into-disorganized-attachment/

(2017). *How to Deal With a Partner or Spouse Having a Mental Breakdown.* ProfessionalCounseling.com. https://www.professional-counselling.com/helping-your-partner-get-over-a-nervous-breakdown.html

(2022). *What is Disorganized Attachment? 9 Signs of The Lesser-Known Attachment Style.* Mind Body Green Mindfulness.

https://www.mindbodygreen.com/articles/disorganized-attachment

(n.d.). *Managing a Relationship Breakdown*. Better Health Channel. https://www.betterhealth.vic.gov.au/health/healthyliving/Managing-a-relationship-breakdown

(n.d.). *How to Handle Someone Who Likes to Play Hot and Cold*. Askmen. https://in.askmen.com/sex-and-dating/1123668/article/how-to-handle-someone-who-likes-to-play-hot-and-cold

(2017). *'I'll Never Vent to a Friend About My Relationship Again - Here's Why'*. Women's Health. https://www.womenshealthmag.com/relationships/a19977024/venting-about-your-relationship/

(2021). *Self-Regulation Tips for Disorganized Attachment Triggers*. The Attachment Project. https://www.attachmentproject.com/blog/self-regulation-disorganized-attachment-triggers/

(2019). *4 Steps to Help You Heal From Disorganized Attachment Style So That You Can Feel Securely Attached In Your Relationships*. Jessica Lang Therapy. https://jessicalangtherapy.com/blog/disorganized-attachment/

(2022). *What To Do If You Have A Disorganized Attachment*. ReGain.

https://www.regain.us/advice/attachment/what-to-do-if-you-have-a-disorganized-attachment/

(2022). *How to Heal Disorganized Attachment in Adults (2022(.* Briana MacWilliam. https://brianamacwilliam.com/heal-disorganized-attachment/

(2022). *How to Improve Your Self Worth.* Nigerian Tribune Online. https://tribuneonlineng.com/how-to-improve-your-self-worth/

(n.d.). *25 Killer Actions to Boost Your Self-Confidence.* Zen Habits. https://zenhabits.net/25-killer-actions-to-boost-your-self-confidence/

(2022). *Why You May Have Trust Issues and How to Overcome Them.* VeryWellMind. https://www.verywellmind.com/why-you-may-have-trust-issues-and-how-to-overcome-them-5215390

(2022). *How to Overcome Trust Issues in a Relationship.* wikiHow. https://www.wikihow.com/Overcome-Trust-Issues-in-a-Relationship

(2022). *Secure Attachment Style in Relationships Explained.* Cosmopolitan UK. https://www.cosmopolitan.com/uk/love-sex/relationships/

(2022). *How to Develop a Secure Attachment Style So That You Can Have Healthier, More Loving Relationships.* Insider Reviews.

https://www.insider.com/guides/health/sex-relationships/secure-attachment

(2022). *Secure Attachment Style: What It Is, Signs, and How to Develop It.* The Truly Charming. https://thetrulycharming.com/secure-attachment/

(n.d.). *What Does a Healthy Relationship Look Like?* NewYork.gov. https://www.ny.gov/teen-dating-violence-awareness-and-prevention/what-does-healthy-relationship-look

(n.d.). *Good Will Hunting.* IMDb. https://www.imdb.com/title/tt0119217/

Printed in Great Britain
by Amazon

27372308R00098